Learn to Program with JavaScript

A Self-Teaching Guide

Chris Kennedy

Questing Vole Press

Learn to Program with JavaScript: A Self-Teaching Guide
by Chris Kennedy

Editor: Bill Gregory
Proofreader: Diane Yee
Compositor: Birgitte Lund
Cover: Questing Vole Press

Contents

CHAPTER 1

Programming Basics

This book explores the core ideas and skills that you'll need when you program with any language on any platform. You can choose from dozens of programming languages, and you'll see many of them here—languages like JavaScript, C, and Python. You'll learn what these different languages are good at and why you might choose one over another. This book won't make you an expert on any one of them but you'll see what all these languages have in common.

By the end of this book, you'll be comfortable approaching any programming language. You'll learn how to:

- Make sense of programming jargon
- Work with variables, conditions, loops, arrays, and more
- Control the structure and the flow of a program
- Create and call functions
- Create and run programs
- Understand programs that other people have written
- Debug programs

What You Need to Know

Few skills are needed to start programming:

- **No required platform.** You can work on Windows, macOS, Linux, or any full-strength operating system (mobile operating systems like iOS and Android aren't suitable for writing programs). You should know your way around your computer and your chosen operating system and web browser.

- **No required programming experience.** If you've never written a line of code, that's fine. If you don't know where to *begin* to write a line of code, that's fine too. If you've written some code but are unsure of the basics, then this is the place to review those fundamentals.

- **No required background.** Schoolteachers, engineers, plumbers, artists, heiresses, sidewalk entertainers, retirees, ten-year-olds—people of every age and walk of life can learn to program.

Programming is a powerful skill. As you progress through this book, don't try to understand everything perfectly. Like mathematics, programming is a deep subject that rewards repeated practice. If you feel like you've picked up 80% of a particular topic, then move on. You can always circle back later. In any case, you'll never achieve complete mastery. Some time months or years from now, you'll return to a program or concept and discover subtle new points and clever efficiencies. It's an experience that everyone shares when they start creating programs rather than merely using them.

Downloading the Example Files

To follow along with the examples in this book, download the companion files from *questingvolepress.com*. Click the link for this book, download the ZIP archive learning_to_program.zip, and then expand it on your desktop (or wherever you like). Inside that folder, each relevant chapter has its own folder where you'll find example files to work with. These files are a convenience; they're not actually required to understand the material.

What is Programming?

You might have heard the phrase "a computer program is a set of instructions." This phrase is technically true but a bit broad. If you've played a 3D video game, created an Excel spreadsheet, sent an email, watched a video, or edited a picture in Photoshop, then you probably weren't left thinking, "That's just a set of instructions."

But that's exactly what every program is: a sequence of small, discrete commands, one after the other. A program can contain three instructions, or three thousand, or three million or more. Each instruction tells the computer to perform a specific operation. The art and challenge of programming is to break apart large tasks into these individual steps. That's not an abstract concept—it's something that everyone does every day.

Suppose that a friend calls you asking for directions to your house. He's at a nearby convenience store that you pass every day on your way home. The entire route pops into your head instantly but you must break it down into simple instructions from point A to point B. So you recite specific, individual, clear steps:

```
turn left
drive straight one mile
turn right on Pearl Street
take the third left
it's the second house on the right
```

The correct sequence is necessary. The instructions:

```
turn left
drive straight one mile
```

take the driver to a place different from:

```
drive straight one mile
turn left
```

If you string together enough of these simple instructions (turn right, walk two miles east, go straight, take a ferry to Stockholm), then they could take you on a years-long trip visiting every national park around the world. Instructions like "take a ferry to Stockholm" can be further subdivided into simpler steps if necessary.

Similarly, when you program you give directions to the computer by breaking apart complex tasks into small, individual instructions and then writing those instructions in a programming language. But rather than "turn right" and "drive straight," computer instructions are commands like:

```
display the letter "A" on the screen
check whether the user just pressed the Enter key
add two numbers
change the color of a specific pixel
```

Starting from the simple programs that you write when you're learning to program, it might be hard to imagine how to get from such basic examples to complex games and applications. But huge programs are the result of massive efforts. It takes hundreds of people working years of fifty-hour weeks writing computer instructions to produce a 3D video game or a Pixar movie.

The enormous speed at which computers execute instructions reveals the limits of human perception. When you play a 3D video game, for example, your computer changes every individual pixel on the screen at least thirty times a second.

Computers do *precisely* what you tell them to do, so the instructions that you give them must make sense. In programming languages, you create these instructions by writing **statements**:

- A statement uses words, numbers, punctuation, and other symbols to describe an instruction.

- The symbols that you use depend on the programming language. Some languages require a semicolon (;) at the end of each statement and others don't, for example. Some languages are strict about uppercase and lowercase letters and others aren't.

- Most statements are short—only a few words and symbols.

Programming itself can be seen as a sequence of steps:

```
form an idea in your mind
break the idea down into its individual pieces
write those pieces in programming language statements
order those statements correctly, using perfect syntax
```

What is a Programming Language?

Hundreds of programming languages exist. Sometimes you get to pick a language and sometimes it's picked for you. At any given time there are perhaps a dozen or so popular languages that:

- Are used by large numbers of people

- Are used to create lots of current software

- Have significant job markets

- Have active online support communities

Languages are a bit like pop singers in this regard. They come and go. They wax and wane in popularity. Some are big hits but most of them aren't. The list of "hot" languages changes slowly, however. Most programmers will learn and use many languages over the course of their career.

Equivalent Statements in a Few Languages

Java
```
score = 100;
```

BASIC
```
LET score = 100
```

AppleScript
```
set score to 100
```

COBOL
```
MOVE 100 TO SCORE.
```

Currently Popular Programming Languages

C
C++
C#
Java
JavaScript
Objective-C
Perl
PHP
Python
R
Ruby
Swift
Visual Basic

Additional languages become easier to pick up after learning the basics. In later chapters, we'll look more deeply into some popular languages.

If you're new to programming, you might be wondering why so many languages exist. Why does writing simple computer instructions require more than just one programming language? That "one" language actually does exist: it's called **machine language** or **machine code**, and it's the *only* language that a computer's CPU understands. The CPU (central processing unit) is the chip that's the brain of any computer: server, mainframe, desktop, laptop, mobile phone, game console, smart thermostat, and so on. We might say informally that when we're programming we're writing code the computer understands, but we're not. The CPU doesn't understand C or JavaScript or Python or any other non-machine language. Machine language programs are the only real instructions that run directly on your computer hardware.

Unfortunately, writing and maintaining machine code is a struggle. Each tiny instruction performs a highly specific operation such as loading data, jumping elsewhere in the program, or moving a unit of data in memory. Machine code is for machines, not people. Even if you did write it, almost no one else would be able to read it (*you* might not be able to read your own code after a few days absence). And because machine code is CPU-specific, you would have to write different machine code for each CPU model. Writing even a trivial machine-code program is so long and tedious a journey that most people never even try.

Consequently, all other programming languages are compromises invented to bridge the gap between humans and computer hardware. Some languages are actually quite close to machine code—the closest is called assembly language. In general, the closer a language is to machine code, the harder it is to write and the more you have to know about the hardware. **Low-level languages** are closer to the hardware than **high-level languages** are. Code written in high-level languages is often easier to write and to share across different operating systems, but tends to run more slowly because these languages aren't necessarily optimized down to the CPU level. Speed differences are often minimal these days, so this book emphasizes high-level languages.

Statements written in C, Java, Python, JavaScript, or any other language are called **source code**, which at some point must be converted into machine code to run on the computer. When someone says that they're coding or programming, they mean that they're writing source code. To start writing source code in any programming language, you must know:

- How to write it (literally, where to start typing)

- How the source code will be converted into machine code

- How to run (execute) it

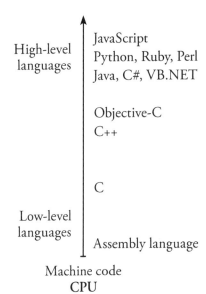

Example Machine Code

```
f8b5 9e55 2a01 0000 0000
0000 0000 0000 4144 5641
5049 3332 2e64 6c6c 004b
4552 4e45 4c33 322e 646c
6c00 4e54 444c 4c2e 444c
4c00 4744 4933 322e 646c
6c00 5553 4552 3332 2e64
6c6c 006d 7376 6372 742e
646c 6c00 434f 4d44 4c47
3332 2e64 6c6c 0053 4845
4c4c 3332 2e64 6c6c 0057
494e 5350 4f4f 4c2e 4452
```

High-level languages — JavaScript Python, Ruby, Perl Java, C#, VB.NET

Objective-C C++

C

Low-level languages — Assembly language

Machine code CPU

Writing Source Code

Programming language source code is written in plain text. You can write in any programming language by using a simple text editor like Notepad on a Windows PC or TextEdit on a Mac. Plain text contains only printable letters, numbers, punctuation, and other symbols—no fonts, formatting, invisible codes, colors, graphics, or any of the clutter usually associated with word processors. If you see a formatting bar with bold and italic buttons, then you're probably using the wrong editor or mode. If you're using an editor that can work in either Rich Text or Plain Text mode (such as TextEdit on a Mac), then use Plain Text.

Filename extensions are used to indicate the programming language—.js for JavaScript files, .c for C files, and .py for Python files, for example—but source code files are no different from plain text (.txt) files.

In many high-level languages, a single statement is all that's needed to write a complete (albeit trivial) program. The "Hello, world!" program is the classic example that's used to illustrate to beginning programmers the basic syntax for constructing a minimal, working program. This program simply prints the words "Hello, world!" on the screen.

C and C-style languages such as C# ("C sharp"), C++ ("C plus plus"), and Java require what at first appears to be an intimidating number of curly braces and obscure keywords just to print "Hello, world!"

Here's "Hello, world!" in C:

```
#include <stdio.h>
main()
{
  printf("Hello, world!");
}
```

And in C#:

```
using System;
public class HelloWorld
{
  public static void Main()
  {
    Console.WriteLine("Hello, world!");
  }
}
```

And in Java:

```
public class HelloWorld {
  public static void main(String[] args) {
    System.out.println("Hello, world!");
  }
}
```

"Hello, world!" in a Few High-Level Languages

JavaScript
```
alert("Hello, world!");
```

Perl
```
say "Hello, world!";
```

Python
```
print "Hello, world!"
```

Ruby
```
puts 'Hello, world!'
```

You don't have to remember all this information just to write a simple program. Even though you *can* work in a basic text editor like Notepad or TextEdit, you almost certainly won't want to because they leave you completely on your own when writing code. Other specialized applications make life easier by actually helping you write code.

Programmer's text editors are plain text editors with extra features. Many free and paid programmer's editors are available on every platform, and some have been around for decades. Typical features include line numbering, advanced find and replace, custom plugins, and multifile project management. Syntax color-coding, which isn't the same as formatting, helps you read and recognize different parts of the language. Syntax checking, analogous to spell checking in a word processor, flags syntax errors in your code as you're actually typing it. Some editors are oriented toward a particular language whereas others support dozens of languages. Popular programmer's editors include Sublime Text, Notepad++, TextWrangler, Vim, and Emacs. Web development applications have programmer's editors for web-specific languages like JavaScript and HTML.

Integrated Development Environments (IDEs) are large programs that include not only a programmer's text editor but many additional features for professional developers. Popular IDEs include Apple's Xcode for macOS, Microsoft's Visual Studio for Windows, and the cross-platform Eclipse IDE.

For the examples in this book, you can use a plain text editor but consider using a programmer's text editor, which offers major advantages over a plain text editor in return for a bit of extra learning. You won't need an IDE until you concentrate on a particular area of development.

Compiled and Interpreted Languages

You have several ways to convert source code into machine code to run your program. Choosing one of these methods is a decision that you'll rarely if ever have to make because most languages use one particular method. Consider the simple scenario where I want to run on my computer a program (source code) that you wrote on your computer.

- **Compiled.** You write source code and then use a program called a **compiler** that accepts your source code and creates from it a separate file that contains machine code. Then, you give me that machine-code file, which is called an **executable** or an **executable file** because I can execute (run) it directly on my computer. I never see your source code.

- **Interpreted.** You give me a copy of your source code file. To run your program on my computer, I need an **interpreter**. An interpreter, unlike a compiler, runs programs on the fly. Think of an interpreter as stepping through source code line by line, processing as it goes. No separate machine-code file is saved. If you've ever visited a website that uses JavaScript (which most of them do these days), then you've used an interpreter. The JavaScript source code is sent from a web server to your computer over the internet (along with webpages, images, videos, and other files). Your web browser interprets that JavaScript to run the code.

Favored Compilation Methods

Compiled
    C
    C++
    Objective-C
    Swift

Interpreted
    JavaScript
    Perl
    PHP
    R
    Ruby

Hybrid
    C#
    Java
    Python
    VB.NET

- **Hybrid.** The in-between approach is called **just-in-time (JIT) compilation**. This hybrid method is more flexible than compiling code and faster than interpreting it. You compile your source code into an **intermediate language**, also called **bytecode**, which comes as close to machine code as possible while still maintaining portability across many platforms. You distribute the bytecode to the people who need to run your program. They take the final step of converting it to machine code to run on their computers. Bytecode is not human-readable.

In theory, any computer language can use any of the approaches described above, but in practice languages tend to have one strongly preferred method:

- C, C++, and Objective-C are typically compiled languages, so you need a compiler. Compilers can be downloaded for free but they're also built into integrated development environments.

- PHP, JavaScript, and many other so-called scripting languages are usually interpreted.

- C#, Java, Python, and VB.NET use the hybrid approach.

Whether code is compiled or interpreted or somewhere between is rarely the sole reason to choose a particular language, but it's something to consider. If your goal is to write a program that runs at maximum speed on a single platform, then favor a compiled language. If you want to write a program that you can move easily across various platforms, then favor an interpreted language. Much of the time, however, the type of project restricts your choice of language. To build iPhone apps, for example, you must use Swift or Objective-C. Programmers who develop Windows desktop applications, websites, and statistical programs typically must choose from only a small set of suitable languages. After you learn the basics of programming, you'll know how to choose a language, be it compiled, interpreted, or hybrid.

Benefits and drawbacks of compiled and interpreted programs

Feature	Compiled vs. Interpreted Programs
Execution	Compiled programs are ready-to-run executables that require no special software to run on the target platform. An interpreted program requires an interpreter for that language to be on the computer of everyone who runs your program.
Speed	Compiled programs that have been optimized for a CPU run much faster than equivalent interpreted programs, which are generally slower because they must be interpreted every time that they run.
Source code privacy	The source code of compiled programs remains private—you distribute only a machine-language executable file. With interpreted programs, you send source code to everyone who needs to run your program, making your source code effectively public.
Portability	Compiled programs won't run across platforms. An executable that runs on Windows won't run on macOS, and vice versa. The same program needs to be compiled separately for different families of CPUs. With interpreted programs, you don't care about the target computer because you're not providing machine code—you just send the source code and let the other side handle it.
Testing	Compiled code requires an extra compile step every time that you want to test your program. Interpreted code is easier to test because there's no in-between compile step—you just write your source code and then run it, letting the interpreter convert it.
Debugging	When things go wrong, interpreted code can be easier to debug because you always have access to all the source code.

CHAPTER 2

Writing Your First Program

JavaScript is friendly for beginners but isn't only a beginner's language. It's popular, relevant, and widely used by professionals, hobbyists, and students. Many languages meet these criteria—Java and Python are probably the most popular teaching languages—but you can get started with JavaScript without installing anything on your computer. JavaScript isn't the most flexible or powerful language, but it's great for exploring programming concepts, it excels at what it's designed to do, and it's easier to learn than many general-purpose languages. So even if you had a different language in mind, JavaScript is a practical language to know.

Tip: Despite their similar names, Java and JavaScript are different languages that aren't related in any meaningful way.

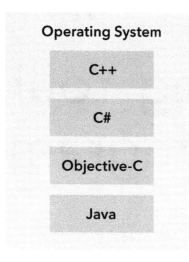

Operating System

C++

C#

Objective-C

Java

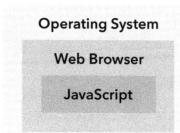

Operating System

Web Browser

JavaScript

Some JavaScript Essentials

The JavaScript language was designed to work with and manipulate web-pages, so it's specialized and intentionally limited. You wouldn't use JavaScript to write a desktop application, for example, the way that you would with C++, C#, Objective-C, or Java. Programs that you write in these languages run directly on the operating system. JavaScript doesn't.

While JavaScript is a programming language, it's also a scripting language. And JavaScript, like some other scripting languages, is embedded inside another program. JavaScript works only inside a web browser. Whether your browser is Chrome, Firefox, Safari, Edge, Internet Explorer, or Opera, they all have a JavaScript interpreter inside them (also called a JavaScript engine).

Because JavaScript is an interpreted language (page 8), you don't have to compile it manually to machine code. That conversion is done automatically by the web browser when you run your JavaScript code. So, the operating system runs the web browser and the web browser runs JavaScript.

JavaScript, like most other languages, is case-sensitive, meaning the interpreter considers *myname*, *myName*, and *MYNAME* to be different words. Pay attention to the case of every letter as you type, read, and debug your source code. Case errors are easy to spot in statements like:

```
score = 100;
```

and:

```
SCORE = 100;
```

But they're not immediately obvious in:

```
document.getElementById("para1").style.color = "red";
```

and:

```
document.getElementByID("para1").style.color = "red";
```

The word *Id* has a lowercase *d* in one statement and an uppercase *D* in the other. (The latter statement is wrong and won't work, but don't worry right now about what these statements do.) Maintaining consistent case is such an important habit that experienced programmers tend to do so even when they're using a case-insensitive language.

Here's what JavaScript code looks like in general (again, don't worry about what this code actually does):

```javascript
// show or hide greeting div element
function toggleGreeting() {
  document.getElementById("greetme").onclick = function() {
    if (document.getElementById("greetme").checked) {
      // set property to show div...
      document.getElementById("greeting").style.display = "block";
    } else {
      // ...or hide it
      document.getElementById("greeting").style.display = "none";
    }
  };
  // show greeting on initial page load
  document.getElementById("greeting").style.display = "block";
}

window.onload = function() {
  toggleGreeting();
};
```

The curly braces { } and statements that end with semicolons (;) are clues that a programming language is influenced by the C programming language. C has been around since the early 1970s and is still going strong. It has shaped the look of many of today's most popular languages. Some share the name—C++, C#, and Objective-C—and some don't. Java is a C-style language, as is JavaScript. Knowing one C-style language makes it easier to pick up other C-style languages.

Up and Running with JavaScript

As an interpreted and browser-embedded scripting language, JavaScript is easy to experiment with—you don't have to install a compiler or worry about creating machine-code files. To interpret JavaScript, you use your web browser to open and run a webpage that points to a file containing JavaScript source code. Let's take it step by step.

Tip: The files for this book's exercises are included with the example files, which you can download (page 2). Alternatively, you can create the files yourself in a text editor. Or you can take a hands-off approach and just read the text—every step along the way is described in detail.

To use a web browser to interpret and run JavaScript, we'll need two text files: a webpage (HTML file) and a file that contains JavaScript source code. The webpage simply points to the JavaScript file and nothing more—no need to worry about websites, web servers, graphics, or any other files. The following folder contains these two files:

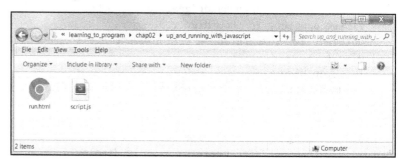

The first file is named run.html. The first part of the name ("run") doesn't matter but the .html file extension is important: double-clicking a .html file opens that file in the default web browser (be it Chrome, Firefox, Safari, or whatever).

The second file, script.js, is a text file that contains JavaScript source code. The name of this file isn't actually important, but it's common practice to use short, lowercase names with the file extension .js (for JavaScript).

Tip: macOS and Windows can be configured to hide file extensions. When you're programming, you should show extensions because they provide valuable information at a glance. For example, if extensions are hidden, then you might think that you're saving a file named script.js when your editor is really saving it as script.js.txt. You can toggle file extensions in Finder Preferences (macOS) or in Folder Options or File Explorer Options (Windows).

Let's look at the contents of the HTML file by opening it in a text editor. Instead of double-clicking run.html, which would open it in a browser, right-click it and then choose Open With > Notepad (Windows) or Open With > TextEdit (macOS). If you like, you can instead use your favorite text editor or web design application. The file run.html contains this HTML code:

```html
<html>
  <head>
    <title>Run script</title>
  </head>
  <body>
    <p>This webpage points to script.js</p>
    <script src="script.js"></script>
  </body>
</html>
```

Tweaking TextEdit on a Mac

TextEdit, the default text editor in macOS, has Rich Text and Plain Text modes. Always write code in plain text: choose TextEdit > Preferences > New Document tab > Plain Text. To make your code align properly from line to line, choose a monospace font such as Monaco, Menlo, or Consolas. Next, click the Open and Save tab and select "Display HTML files as HTML code instead of formatted text". Close Preferences. Finally, disable Smart Quotes and Smart Dashes in Edit > Substitutions.

HTML (Hypertext Markup Language) is the standard markup language used to create webpages. Web browsers read HTML files and render them into webpages. HTML describes the *structure* of a webpage (title, headings, paragraphs, images, and so on), making it a markup language rather than a programming language (HTML code isn't a program or process). The important line here is:

```
<script src="script.js"></script>
```

This line points from this HTML file (this webpage) to what we're really interested in: the JavaScript file named script.js. Because script.js is in the same folder as run.html, we don't have to specify a path (folder location) for script.js. Open script.js in your text editor. It contains one JavaScript statement:

```
alert("Hello, world!");
```

The classic "Hello, world!" program in JavaScript is a single instruction. You can now close both files and quit your text editor.

To run the JavaScript source code, double-click the run.html icon. The webpage opens in your default web browser, which loads script.js, interprets the JavaScript code, and then runs it. The result is a "Hello, world!" message in a JavaScript pop-up alert box. Each browser shows this box slightly differently. Here it is in Google Chrome:

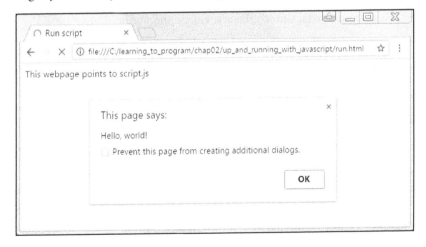

Getting Input

Computer programs accept input, process it, and produce output. In days of yore, programs read input data from punch cards. Nowadays, the sources of input include:

- Characters and commands typed on a keyboard
- Mouse clicks and drags or touchscreen taps and swipes
- Data stored in files
- Spoken commands and dictation
- Values from database and accounting systems
- Button pushes and gyrations from game controllers
- Real-time data streams from robots, cameras, stock tickers, medical and scientific equipment, satellites, and motion and acoustic sensors

Output is equally varied:

- Onscreen text and graphics
- Files and printouts
- Simulated human voices
- Real-time charts, timers, tickers, video, and audio
- Game-controller vibrations and other haptic feedback
- Volume, brightness, and temperature changes
- Automated steering, driving, and equipment adjustments
- Audible alarms and alerts

Different languages favor different types of input and output. JavaScript is all about the web—mainly, what's on webpages and how people interact with webpages.

In the preceding example, we generated output: an alert box with the message "Hello, world!" That's not impressive output, but it's output all the same. Our computer program caused something to happen onscreen.

Let's feed a program some input. We have the same setup as before: two files in a folder. The webpage file, run.html, is identical and exists only to point to the JavaScript file, script.js. The contents of script.js are different this time:

```javascript
var name = prompt("What is your name?");
alert("Hello, " + name);
```

Double-click run.html to open it in your web browser and run the JavaScript code. A prompt box appears onscreen asking "What is your name?" and giving you a place to type. (Again, different browsers display slightly different boxes.) I'll type *Chris* and then click OK. In return, I get an alert box with the message "Hello, Chris".

Tip: Because pop-up dialog boxes are one of JavaScript's most annoying and abused features, some browsers detect them and ask whether you want to prevent the current webpage from creating more of them. Here, you *want* to see them, so be sure not to prevent them.

We have two JavaScript statements. The first statement:

```
var name = prompt("What is your name?");
```

does two things: it uses the JavaScript prompt function to ask for a name and then stores that name in a variable. This variable is a container that can hold data. If we don't store the data, then we won't be able to use it in the next statement.

Usually the JavaScript interpreter processes each statement and then moves immediately to the next statement, but here the prompt function causes the program to pause and wait indefinitely for a response. After somebody types an answer in the prompt box and then clicks OK, three things happen:

- The typed value is stored in a variable named *name*
- The prompt box disappears
- The interpreter runs the next statement

The next statement:

```
alert("Hello, " + name);
```

uses the + operator to combine "Hello," a space, and whatever was typed (the contents of name) and then displays this message in another pop-up box. The prompt function doesn't actually care what you type. You can run this program again and type a sentence, a number, or nothing at all.

Tip: To quickly run a program again by reloading the current webpage, click the browser's Reload or Refresh button C or press the F5 key.

Here, it doesn't matter what you type, but if our program was expecting something specific to work with—like an email address, future date, or purchase amount—then the wrong input could cause the program to crash. The old acronym GIGO, for Garbage In, Garbage Out, applies to programming. In later chapters, you'll see how to check input for correctness.

Tokens

Tokens are the basic indivisible particles of programming languages; they cannot be reduced grammatically by a compiler or interpreter. JavaScript tokens include:

- Variable names (name, x, i, price1, price2, petName)

- Keywords (var, function, if, true, else, null, for)

- Operators (-, *, %, ++, =, !, +=, ==, ===, >, <=, &&, ||)

- Literals (12.34, -5, false, ".com")

- Delimiters (,)

- Escape characters (\', \", \\, \n, \t)

Tokens are assembled into **expressions**, which produce other values, and statements, which are executable lines of source code.

Documenting Your Code

A **comment** is text that you embed in your program source code to explain it. Comments usually describe what a program does and how, but they can also explain why code was changed and give copyright and author information.

The interpreter ignores comments; they are for future programmers who must understand your code to change it.

A single-line comment starts with //. Any text between // and the end of the line is ignored by the JavaScript interpreter (isn't executed):

```
// Change heading
document.getElementById("hdr1").innerHTML = "First Page";
// Change paragraph
document.getElementById("p1").innerHTML = "First paragraph.";
```

You can also use a single-line comment at the end of a line:

```
var count, mean, stdev, min, max;  // Univariate statistics
scores = [88, 69, 85, 94, 74];  // Watch for outliers
```

A multiline comment, also called a comment block, starts with /* and end with */. Any text between /* and */ is ignored by the interpreter:

```
/*
Change the main heading and
the first paragraph in the
current webpage.
*/
document.getElementById("hdr1").innerHTML = "First Page";
document.getElementById("p1").innerHTML = "First paragraph.";
```

For testing and debugging, you can **comment out** (disable) lines of code by converting them to comments temporarily. Adding // in front of a code line changes the line from an executable line to a comment:

```
// document.getElementById("hdr1").innerHTML = "First Page";
```

You can use a comment block to prevent execution of multiple lines:

```
/*
document.getElementById("hdr1").innerHTML = "First Page";
document.getElementById("p1").innerHTML = "First paragraph.";
*/
```

Tip: Exercise restraint when writing comments. A program with too many comments sometimes is as hard to read as a program with none. Don't include obvious explanations such as "Open the file" or "Increment counter".

Using Whitespace

Whitespace includes spaces, tabs, and line breaks—the "blank" characters that represent space between other characters, tokens, and statements.

Like all programming languages, JavaScript permits blank lines, which you should use judiciously; a little whitespace will make your programs easier to read. As it does comments, the JavaScript interpreter ignores blank lines in source code.

The interpreter also ignores multiple spaces. These three statements are equivalent:

```
var person = "Sue";  // Preferred style
var person="Sue";
      var        person        =                "Sue"        ;
```

A good practice is to use spaces to separate operators in expressions and statements. This statement:

```
a = (b + c) && (d != e);  // Preferred style
```

is easier to read than:

```
a=(b+c)&&(d!=e);
```

Because semicolons (;) terminate JavaScript statements, you can place multiple statements on one line. For example, these three statements:

```
a = 2;      // Preferred style
b = 3;
c = a + b;
```

can all be placed on the same line:

```
a = 2; b = 3; c = a + b;
```

Programmers often keep code lines shorter than 80 characters. If a JavaScript statement doesn't fit on one line, the best place to break it is after an operator:

```
document.getElementById("quote").innerHTML =
"Irony is Fate's most common figure of speech.";
```

Don't break lines inside tokens or quoted strings. To insert a line break inside a string, use the escape character \n (page 33). The statement:

```
var name = prompt("What is\nyour name?");
```

displays:

```
What is
your name?
```

See also "Adopting a Programming Style" on page 75.

CHAPTER 3

Variables & Data Types

alice@example.com

email

25000

loanAmount

2018-12-28

invoiceDate

x: 300, y: 20

imagePosition

−123.45

x

Understanding Variables

A **variable** is a named storage location for data. If you write a loan calculator, then you need to keep track of the loan amount, term, interest rate, payments, and number of payments per year. If you write a video game, then you need to keep track of the player's current score, remaining lives, position on the screen, avatar image, and more.

Variables are simply containers or buckets. When you create a variable, you grab a little piece of computer memory and give it a name to use while your program is running. You then put a value in that space, like an email address, a number, a date, or a position. You can change this value as you need to (variables can vary, hence the name).

In JavaScript, you create, or **declare**, a variable by typing the word var in all lowercase letters, followed by the name of the variable:

```
var year;
```

The word var is a JavaScript keyword, meaning it's a built-in part of the language. The name of the variable is up to you and it should represent the value that you want to store, for example:

```
var email;
var loanAmount;
var invoiceDate;
var imagePosition;
var x;
```

Assignment Statements

An assignment statement like:

```
x = 5;
```

can be confusing if you're familiar with only the mathematical meaning of =. In JavaScript, the = operator is a command—it doesn't denote equality. An assignment statement sets the value stored in the storage location denoted by a variable name; in other words, it copies a value into the variable. The *programming* statement:

```
x = x + 1;
```

adds one to the current value of x, but the *mathematical* statement $x = x + 1$ is a false equality.

```
┌─────────────────────┐
│                     │
│      undefined      │
│                     │
└─────────────────────┘
         year
```

```
┌─────────────────────┐
│                     │
│        2018         │
│                     │
└─────────────────────┘
         year
```

If you're experimenting, you can give variables nonsense names:

```
var var1;
var var2;
var foo;
var bar;
```

The name that you give your variable must be written as one word (no spaces) that contains only:

- Letters (a–z, A–Z)

- Digits (0, 1, 2, ..., 9)

- Dollar signs ($)

- Underscores (_)

No other characters are allowed, and names can't begin with a digit. This variable name, for example, won't work:

```
var 10examples;  // Invalid name
```

Placing the number at the end works:

```
var examples10;  // Valid name
```

All that declaring a variable does is claim a named area of memory to hold a value. When this statement runs:

```
var year;
```

the variable named *year* springs into existence but has no value, meaning the state of this variable is **undefined**.

There's no point to declaring a variable that stays undefined. The equal sign (=), called the **assignment operator**, puts a value in a variable. You can set the value of a variable by using two statements:

```
var year;
year = 2018;
```

Or you can use a single statement that both declares the variable and sets its initial value:

```
var year = 2018;
```

You can declare multiple variables by using multiple statements:

```
var year;
var month;
var day;
```

Or you can combine them into one, shorthand statement, separating the variable names with commas:

```
var year, month, day;
```

Similarly, you can declare multiple variables and assign them initial values by using multiple statements:

```
var year = 2018;
var month = 12;
var day = 20;
```

or one statement:

```
var year = 2018, month = 12, day = 28;
```

See also "Adopting a Programming Style" on page 75.

Strong and Weak Typing

In JavaScript, after you've declared a variable, you can store any value in it. You can start by putting a number in a variable, then put a date in it later in your program, and then put text in it still later. But many other languages won't let you do this: when you declare a variable, you must name it and define what *type* of data it can hold. You must decide beforehand if a variable is going to store:

- An integer (zero or a positive or negative whole number with no decimal point)

- A floating-point number (a real number with a decimal point dividing the real and fractional parts)

- A single character

- Multiple characters (called a string)

- A boolean value (a value that can be only true or false)

- A more-complex type of data value

After you choose the data type, you can't change it mid-program. Each variable must be of one particular type, and trying to store the wrong type of data in a variable will cause an error that stops the program. Languages that enforce this behavior are called **strongly typed languages**.

JavaScript, because it doesn't enforce variable types, is a **weakly typed language**. After declaring a variable:

```
var myVar;
```

you can set it to different types of values without restriction:

```
myVar = 100;            // A number
myVar = "abc";          // A string
myVar = true;           // A boolean value
myVar = [1, 2, 3, 4];   // An array
myVar = new Date();     // A Date object
```

Always Use var

The keyword var isn't actually required to create a variable. JavaScript lets you create one on the fly without it:

```
year = 2018;
```

This statement causes JavaScript to look for an existing variable named *year* to assign it the value 2018, but if it doesn't find year, it will just create it. That's sloppy programming, however. You should always use var to create variables because omitting it can lead to unexpected behavior and hard-to-find errors. For example, recall that JavaScript is case-sensitive, so the statements:

```
var x = 100;
X = 101;
```

create two different variables, named *x* and *X*. Maybe the second line has an error—you meant to type a lowercase *x*. But because the var-less uppercase *X* was created automatically, you now have two different variables that JavaScript isn't going to warn you about.

Assigning a value to a variable that hasn't been declared with var can also cause scope problems (page 57).

Surround a string value with quotes to specify where it begins and ends. JavaScript lets you use either double quotes or single quotes, but don't mix them (page 33). You can't start a string with a double quote and close it with a single quote, for example. I prefer to use double quotes because that's more common in other languages.

A boolean value is a value that's either true or false. The lowercase words `true` and `false` are part of the JavaScript language and don't need quotes.

Despite its generic nature of variable storage, JavaScript treats values of different types differently. Numbers are treated differently from strings and strings are treated differently from boolean values. JavaScript variables can also hold more-complex values such as functions, arrays, and objects, which are covered in later chapters.

Weak typing may sound attractive because you can store anything anywhere, but problems can arise when there's no guarantee that a variable contains the type of data you think it does. In most of your programming, you won't need or want to change the type of data that a variable stores. If you have a variable named *price*, then you would expect it to contain a number, not the string `"nutmeg"` or the boolean value `false`. If you have a variable named *lastName*, then you don't want it to contain the numeric value `123.45`. Strongly typed languages have internal rules that prevent common errors like these. JavaScript doesn't.

JavaScript Reserved Words

JavaScript has a number of reserved words that can't be used as names of variables, functions, or other objects:

abstract	arguments	boolean	break	byte
case	catch	char	class	const
continue	debugger	default	delete	do
double	else	enum	eval	export
extends	false	final	finally	float
for	function	goto	if	implements
import	in	instanceof	int	interface
let	long	native	new	null
package	private	protected	public	return
short	static	super	switch	synchronized
this	throw	throws	transient	true
try	typeof	var	void	volatile
while	with	yield		

Working with Numbers

The most common type of values in computer programs is numeric values. In many programming languages, you must pay attention to the types of numbers that you're dealing with: whether they're integers or floating-point numbers, whether they're positive or negative or zero, and whether they're large or small in magnitude. JavaScript instead takes a more human approach to numbers: it has only one type of number, and numbers can be written with or without decimal points. Here are some examples:

```
var a, b, c, d, e, f, g, h;
a = 0;              // Zero (integer)
b = 5;              // Positive integer (no decimal point)
c = -100;           // Negative integer
d = -1234567;       // No thousands separators in large numbers
e = 123.456;        // Floating-point number
f = 2.5e2;          // Scientific notation (250)
g = -2.5e-2;        // Scientific notation (-0.025)
h = 0.000000034;    // Displayed as 3.4e-8
```

Numbers, unlike strings, aren't surrounded by quotes. The numbers in the preceding examples are **numeric literals** that represent fixed values.

As we did with strings in Chapter 2, we can display numbers in an alert box. To display the value of the variable b, for example, run the statement `alert(b);`:

Don't surround the variable name with quotes. You want to display the *value* of the variable named *b*. The statement `alert("b");` would display the letter *b*.

See also "Converting a String to a Number" on page 62.

Floating-Point Numbers

Floating-point numbers represent real numbers and are written with a decimal point separating the integer and fractional parts. A number in **scientific notation** is written as a decimal number multiplied by an integer power of 10. An *E* or *e* is the exponentiation symbol: $2.5e2 = 2.5 \times 10^2 = 250$, for example. The **mantissa** is the portion that expresses the significant digits (2.5 here), and the **exponent** is the power of 10 (2 here). The mantissa and exponent each can have a sign: $-2.5e-2 = -2.5 \times 10^{-2} = -2.5 \times 0.01 = -0.025$.

Operand	Operator	Operand
x	+	2

Unary arithmetic operators

Operator	What It Does
-x	Reverses the sign of *x*
+x	Leaves *x* unchanged
x++	Adds one to *x*
x--	Subtracts one from *x*

Binary arithmetic operators

Operator	What It Does
x + y	Sums *x* and *y*
x - y	Subtracts *y* from *x*
x * y	Multiplies *x* and *y*
x / y	Divides *x* by *y*
x % y	Remainder of *x* / *y*

Basic Arithmetic

A **unary arithmetic operator** performs a mathematical operation on a single numeric operand to produce a result. The – (negation) operator changes the sign of its operand, and the + (plus) operator leaves its operand unchanged. Adding one and subtracting one are common programming operations, so JavaScript provides the shorthand ++ (increment) and –– (decrement) operators.

```
var x = 5;
var y = -3;
var z = x + y;   // 2
x--;             // 4  (same as x = x - 1)
y++;             // -2 (same as y = y + 1)
alert("z = " + z + ", x = " + x + ", y = " + y);
```

This page says:

z = 2 x = 4 y = -2

☐ Prevent this page from creating additional dialogs.

OK

A **binary arithmetic operator** performs a mathematical operation on two numeric operands to produce a result. These operators include the usual ones: + (addition), – (subtraction), * (multiplication), and / (division). The following code calculates a loan repayment with simple interest.

```
var principal = 1000;
var interestRate = 0.07125;
var interest, payment;
interest = principal * interestRate;
payment = principal + interest;
alert("payment = " + payment);   // 1071.25
```

This page says:

payment = 1071.25

☐ Prevent this page from creating additional dialogs.

OK

Tip: In technical terms, JavaScript numbers are stored as 64-bit (double-precision) floating-point numbers, following the international IEEE 754 standard.

Raising a Number to a Power

JavaScript doesn't have an exponentiation operator (in other languages, this operator is commonly ^ or **). Instead, you must use the pow() method to raise a number to a power. pow() is a method of the Math object (page 30). The expression Math.pow(x,y)—or, mathematically, x^y—shows how many times the **base**, x, is multiplied by the **exponent**, y. A positive exponent indicates multiplication ($2^4 = 2 \times 2 \times 2 \times 2$), a negative exponent indicates division ($2^{-4} = 1/2^4$), and a fractional exponent indicates a root of the base ($16^{1/2} = 4$ = the square root of 16).

```
var a = Math.pow(0, 1);      // 0
var b = Math.pow(2, 3);      // 8
var c = Math.pow(2, -3);     // 0.125
var d = Math.pow(-3, 3);     // -27
var e = Math.pow(25, 0.5);   // 5 (square root of 25)
var f = Math.pow(27, 1/3);   // 3 (cube root of 27)
```

Prefix and Postfix Expressions

The ++ (increment) operator adds one to its operand and returns a value. If used **prefix**, with operator before operand (++x, for example), then the expression returns the value *after* incrementing. If used **postfix**, with operator after operand (x++, for example), then the expression returns the value *before* incrementing.

```
// Prefix
var a = 2;
b = ++a; // b = 3, a = 3

// Postfix
var x = 2;
y = x++; // y = 2, x = 3
```

The —— (decrement) operator, which subtracts one from its operand, works similarly.

To avoid errors related to prefix and postfix usage, don't increment variables in assignment statements. Write two separate statements.

Getting the Remainder of a Division

The % (modulo) operator yields the remainder of a division. 20 % 6 is 2 because 20 equals 3 * 6 + 2. You usually perform **modular division** to check whether one number is evenly divisible by another. If x % 2 is 0, for example, then x is even. You can also use modular division to scale numbers to a desired range. If x is a random integer, then (x % 6) + 1 will always be between 1 and 6, inclusive (the roll of a die, perhaps). Here's another trick: x % 10^n returns the n rightmost digits of x. Modular division is usually performed on integers, but JavaScript permits floating-point numbers too. 2.4 % 0.7 is 0.3, for example, because 2.4 equals 3 * 0.7 + 0.3.

```
var a = 10 % 3;        // 1
var b = 10 % 4;        // 2
var c = 10 % 5;        // 0
var d = 10 % 6;        // 4
var e = 15 % 4;        // 3
var f = -15 % 4;       // -3
var g = 15 % -4;       // 3
var h = -15 % -4;      // -3
var i = 1234567890 % (Math.pow(10, 5));   // 67890
var j = 1.7 % 0.5;     // 0.19999999999999996
var k = 2 % 0.4;       // 0.3999999999999999
var l = 0 % 10;        // 0
```

Roundoff Errors

Sometimes, operations on floating-point numbers produce results that differ from what you expect. For example, if you run:

```
var x = 0.1 + 0.2;
```

then the resulting x is 0.30000000000000004 rather than the expected 0.3. This difference occurs because JavaScript (like C, Java, Python, and other languages) uses internal binary (base 2) representations of decimal (base 10) numbers. Unfortunately, most decimal fractions can't be represented exactly in binary, so small differences occur. This difference is called **representation error** or **roundoff error**. This design tradeoff (speed versus accuracy) isn't generally considered to be a bug. JavaScript rounds floating-point numbers to 17 significant digits, which is enough precision for most applications.

Here's a trick to apply to the example above: multiply each of the two numbers by 10 to convert them to integers (which are represented exactly), and then divide their sum by 10:

```
var x = (0.1 * 10 + 0.2 * 10) / 10;
```

The resulting x is 0.3.

Integers are accurate up to 15 digits:

```
var a = 999999999999999;    // a will be 999999999999999
var b = 9999999999999999;   // b will be 10000000000000000
```

Controlling Calculation Order

The calculation order of arithmetic expressions is determined by precedence and associativity. **Precedence** determines the priority of various operators when more than one is used in an expression. Operations with higher precedence are performed first. The expression 2 + 3 * 4 is 14 rather than 20 because multiplication has higher precedence than addition. JavaScript first computes 3 * 4 and then adds 2.

Associativity determines the order of evaluation in an expression when adjacent operators have equal precedence. JavaScript uses left-to-right associativity for arithmetic expressions. The * and / operators have the same precedence, so 6 / 2 * 3 is 9 (not 1) because 6 / 2 is evaluated first.

You can use parentheses to override precedence and associativity. Expressions inside parentheses are evaluated before expressions outside them. Adding parentheses to the preceding examples, you get (2 + 3) * 4 is 20 and 6 / (2 * 3) is 1. It's good programming style to add parentheses to long expressions to increase readability.

Tip: The ++ (increment) and −− (decrement) operators have higher precedence than the unary + (plus) and − (negation) operators. If x is 4, then −−x is 3, not −(−4) = 4.

Arithmetic operator precedence (highest to lowest)

Operator	Description
+x, -x	Unary plus, unary negation
*, /, %	Multiplication, division, modulo
+, -	Addition, subtraction

The Math Object

You can use the properties and methods of the built-in Math object to do other common mathematical calculations (objects are covered in Chapter 11). You can refer to the constant pi (π) as Math.PI, for example, or calculate the sine function of x as Math.sin(x). Constants are defined with the full precision of floating-point numbers.

```javascript
var a = Math.PI;            // 3.141592653589793
var b = Math.E;             // 2.718281828459045
var c = Math.abs(-4);       // 4
var d = Math.ceil(6.4);     // 7
var e = Math.ceil(-5.5);    // -5
var f = Math.floor(4.7);    // 4
var g = Math.floor(-5.5);   // -6
var h = Math.max(0, 150, 30, 20, -8, -200);    // 150
var i = Math.min(0, 150, 30, 20, -8, -200);    // -200

// Return a random floating-point number between 0 and 1
var j = Math.random();

// Return a random integer between 0 and 10
var k = Math.floor(Math.random() * 11);

var l = Math.round(2.7);    // 3
var m = Math.round(2.4);    // 2
var n = Math.sqrt(16);      // 4
var o = Math.sqrt(3);       // 1.7320508075688772
```

Math object properties (mathematical constants)

Property	Description
E	Euler's constant e and the base of the natural logarithm, approximately 2.718.
LN2	Natural logarithm of 2, approximately 0.693.
LN10	Natural logarithm of 10, approximately 2.303.
LOG2E	Base 2 logarithm of e, approximately 1.443.
LOG10E	Base 10 logarithm of e, approximately 0.434.
PI	Ratio of the circumference of a circle to its diameter, approximately 3.14159.
SQRT1_2	Square root of 1/2; equivalently, 1 over the square root of 2, approximately 0.707.
SQRT2	Square root of 2, approximately 1.414.

Math object methods (mathematical functions)

Method	Description
abs(x)	Returns the absolute value of x (the positive distance between x and zero).
acos(x)	Returns the arccosine of x. The result is between 0 and π radians.
asin(x)	Returns the arcsine of x. The result is between $-\pi/2$ and $\pi/2$ radians.
atan(x)	Returns the arctangent of x. The result is between $-\pi/2$ and $\pi/2$ radians.
atan2(y,x)	Returns the arctangent of the quotient y/x. The result is between $-\pi$ and π radians.
ceil(x)	Returns the smallest integer not less than x.
cos(x)	Returns the cosine of x radians. The result is between -1 and 1.
exp(x)	Returns e^x, where e is Euler's constant (2.718...), the base of the natural logarithm.
floor(x)	Returns the largest integer not greater than x.
log(x)	Returns the natural logarithm (ln) of x, for $x > 0$.
max(x,y,z,...)	Returns the number with the highest value.
min(x,y,z,...)	Returns the number with the lowest value.
pow(x,y)	Returns the value of x to the power of y.
random()	Returns a floating-point random number between 0 (inclusive) and 1 (exclusive).
round(x)	Returns the value of x rounded to the nearest integer.
sin(x)	Returns the sine of x radians. The result is between -1 and 1.
sqrt(x)	Returns the positive square root of x, for $x \geq 0$.
tan(x)	Returns the tangent of x radians.

Operator	Assigns This Value to x
x += y	*x* incremented by *y*
x -= y	*x* decremented by *y*
x *= y	*x* multiplied by *y*
x /= y	*x* divided by *y*
x %= y	Remainder of *x* / *y*

Making Arithmetic Assignments

Assignment expressions such as x = x + 1 are so common that JavaScript provides a shortcut assignment operator for each binary arithmetic operator (page 26). The expression x += 1 is equivalent to x = x + 1, for example.

The expression x *op* y is evaluated as x *op* (y), where *op* is any assignment operator. For example, the statement:

```
x *= y + 1;
```

is equivalent to:

```
x = x * (y + 1);
```

and not:

```
x = (x * y) + 1;
```

Tip: To add or subtract one, you can use the ++ (increment) or −− (decrement) operator instead of an arithmetic assignment. Use x-- instead of x -= 1, for example.

```
var a = 5;
var b = 5;
var c = 5;
var d = 5;
var e = 5;
var x = 2;
a += x + 1;     // 8
b -= x + 1;     // 2
c *= x + 1;     // 15
d /= x + 1;     // 1.6666666666666667
e %= x + 1;     // 2
```

The assignment statements x = x + 1 and x += 1 execute identically. From a programmer's point of view, it looks like the latter statement is more efficient because the former statement computes x twice: once when it evaluates the right-side x and again when it assigns the result to the left-side x. Whereas the latter expression computes x only once or *in place*, meaning that JavaScript saves time and memory by modifying only the original x. The interpreter recognizes these statements as identical, however, and generates the same machine code for both. That said, you should use the += form because it's easier to read and less prone to syntax errors.

Working with Strings

Here's a string: `"Follow me!"` Here's another one: `""`. A **string** is a sequence of zero of more characters surrounded by quotes. The quotes tell JavaScript to treat the characters as a single item, so you can't embed comments, extra white space, or anything else that you don't want to be part of the string. You use strings to handle text in your programs: characters, words, sentences, paragraphs, names, email addresses, and so on.

A value that's surrounded by quotes is called a **string literal**. (A constant number such as 3 or –123.45 is called a numeric literal.) The first line of code that we wrote was this alert message that used a string literal:

```
alert("Hello, world!");
```

Variables can contain strings. The following statement declares a new variable named *message* and sets it equal to the string "Hello, world!".

```
var message = "Hello, world!";
```

You can then use that variable to display the value of `message` in an alert box:

```
alert(message);
```

Be sure not to put quotes around `message` in the preceding statement. The statement:

```
alert("message");
```

would print the word "message", which isn't what you want. You want to print the value of the variable named *message*.

You can enclose a string in double quotes or single quotes:

```
var myString1 = "Double quotes work.";      // OK
var myString2 = 'Single quotes also work.'; // OK
```

The same type of quote that starts a string literal must end it. You can't open with a double quote and close with a single quote, for example:

```
var myString3 = "Mixed quotes will not work.'; // Wrong
```

Most other programming languages permit only double-quoted strings, so I tend to use double quotes in JavaScript to make it easier to move from language to language.

For quotes inside quotes, you can embed double quotes in a single-quoted string, and vice versa. Suppose that you want to create a string that contains the phrase "Don't worry." You can't use single quotes to start and end the string because there's also a single quote in the middle of the string, and JavaScript would interpret this middle quote as the end of the string:

```
var phrase1 = 'Don't worry.'; // Wrong
```

Escape characters

Character	Description
\\	Backslash (one \)
\'	Single quote (one ')
\"	Double quote (one ")
\n	New line (or line feed)
\r	Carriage return (different from \n)
\t	Tab
\b	Backspace
\f	Form feed (new page)

Instead, use double quotes with a single quote contained inside them:

```
var phrase1 = "Don't worry.";  // OK
```

There's no simple way to mark the start and end of a more-complex string that contains both double quotes and single quotes:

```
var phrase2 = "He said, "Don't worry," and left.";  // Wrong
```

Here, you'll need to use **escape characters** (or **escape sequences**) for characters that would cause JavaScript to misinterpret the string literal. An escape character starts with a backslash (\). The escape character for a double quote is \" and for a single quote is \'. This technique is called *escaping the quotes*:

```
var phrase2 = "He said, \"Don't worry,\" and left.";  // OK
```

If JavaScript doesn't recognize an escape character, then it leaves the character following the backslash unchanged. The expression alert("\w"), for example, prints "w" (without the quotes).

For more information about working with strings, see Chapter 6.

CHAPTER 4

Conditional Code

Boolean Values

The Hello World-level programs that we've written so far are the simplest type of programs: the JavaScript interpreter starts at the first statement, executes it, moves to the next statement, executes it, and so on until the last line of the program. The interpreter pauses if the program prompts the user for information (input), but still moves from top to bottom, executing each line in sequential order without exceptions. Real-world programs are never this trivial. They run code based on whether specified conditions are true or false at the time of execution:

- Is the bank balance is positive?
- Did the user check a box on the form?
- Did the missile hit the spaceship?
- Is the temperature above freezing?

To write conditional code, you'll need a data type that can have only one of two values, like:

- Yes/No
- On/Off
- Succeed/Fail
- Alive/Dead
- True/False

In programming, a **boolean data type** lets you represent true and false. JavaScript's boolean data type can have only the literal values true or false. Languages that don't have an explicit (built-in) boolean data type use numbers or integers to represent boolean values: zero if false, and nonzero or one if true.

A **boolean expression** (also called a logical expression or conditional expression) evaluates to one of two states: true or false, called **boolean values** (or truth values). Boolean values are complementary: "true" means "not false." In JavaScript, a false expression evaluates to one of the following values. Consequently, a true expression evaluates to any value not listed below.

- 0 (zero)

- -0 (minus zero)

- "" (empty string)

- false (the boolean literal value false)

- An undefined value

- NaN (Not-a-Number, page 62)

- null (a null value)

```
var a = 0;              // false (zero)
var b = -0;             // false (minus zero)
var c = -100;           // true (nonzero)
var d = 3.14;           // true (nonzero)
var e = "";             // false (empty string)
var f = " ";            // true (nonempty string - a space)
var g = "Hello";        // true (nonempty string)
var h = "false";        // true (nonempty string)
var i = false;          // false (boolean literal)
var j = true;           // true (boolean literal)
var k;                  // false (undefined value)
var l = Math.sqrt(-1);  // false (Not-a-Number)
var m = 10 / "A";       // false (Not-a-Number)
var n = null;           // false (null value)
```

Logical Operators

Logical operators (or boolean operators) are used with boolean values to make decisions based on conditions. JavaScript's logical operators are:

- ! (called the "not" operator, or logical negation)

- && (called the "and" operator, or logical conjunction)

- || (called the "or" operator, or logical inclusion)

The ! (not) operator takes a single operand and negates, or inverts, its boolean value. This operator returns true if its operand is false, or false otherwise.

```
var a = 0;
var b = 1.5;
var c = "";
var d = "Hello";
var e = false;
var f = true;
!a;        // true
!b;        // false
!c;        // true
!d;        // false
!e;        // true
!f;        // false
!("abc");  // false
!(123);    // false
```

The && and || operators actually return the value of one of the specified operands, so if these operators are used with nonboolean values, then they may return a nonboolean value. x && y returns x if x is false, or y otherwise. x || y returns y if x is false, or x otherwise. The results of logical operations are summarized in the following table (the operands x and y represent expressions).

Results of logical operations

x	y	x && y	x || y	!x
false	false	x (or false)	y (or false)	true
true	false	y (or false)	x (or true)	false
false	true	x (or false)	y (or true)	
true	true	y (or true)	x (or true)	

The && (and) operator takes two operands and performs a left-to-right evaluation to determine whether *both* operands are true. JavaScript won't evaluate the right operand if the expression's truth value is determined by the left operand. If x is false, for example, then x && y evaluates and returns x and ignores y, no matter what its value is.

The || (or) operator takes two operands and performs a left-to-right evaluation to determine whether *either* operand is true. As with &&, JavaScript won't evaluate the right operand if the expression's truth value is determined by the left operand. If x is true, for example, then x || y evaluates and returns x and ignores y, no matter what its value is.

```
var a = true;
var b = false;
var c = 0;
var d = 5;
var e = 8;
var f = "";
var g = "xyz";
a && b;   // false
a || b;   // true
a && a;   // true
b || b;   // false
c && d;   // 0 (false)
c || d;   // 5 (true)
d || c;   // 5 (true)
c || c;   // 0 (false)
d && e;   // 8 (true)
e && d;   // 5 (true)
f && g;   // "" (false)
f || g;   // "xyz" (true)
a || c;   // true
e && a;   // true
a && c;   // 0 (false)
```

Tip: You can assign the result of a boolean expression to a variable. This assignment is commonly used to replace an undefined value with a default value. For example, the expression country = s || "US" assigns country the value "US" if s is "" (or any other false value).

Comparison operators

Operator	Description
==	Equal to
===	Strict equal to
!=	Not equal to
!==	Strict not equal to
<	Less than
<=	Less than or equal to
>	Greater than
>=	Greater than or equal to

Comparison Operators

Comparison operators are used in boolean expressions to test the relation between two values. The way that the values are compared depends on their type. Numbers are compared arithmetically, strings are compared lexicographically (character by character), and booleans are compared logically (true or false).

If the two operands have different types (a number and a string, for example), then JavaScript converts the operands to the same type before making the comparison. When comparing a number and a string, JavaScript converts the string to a number. An empty string converts to zero. A non-numeric string converts to NaN (Not-a-Number, page 62), which always compares as false. When comparing a number and a boolean, the boolean operand is converted to one if it is true or zero if it is false.

To prevent automatic type conversion, use one of the strict comparison operators (=== or !==), which are intended for performing equality comparisons on operands of the same type. The strict equality (===) operator returns true if the operands are strictly equal with no type conversion. The strict inequality operator (!==) returns true if the operands are not equal or not of the same type.

See also "Converting a String to a Number" on page 62 and "Comparing Strings" on page 63.

```
var x = 2;
var y = 0;
var z = true;
var w = "cat";
x == 4        // false
x == 2        // true
x == "2"      // true
x === 2       // true
x === "2"     // false
x != 4        // true
x !== 2       // false
x !== "2"     // true
x !== 4       // true
x > 4         // false
x < 4         // true
x >= 4        // false
x <= 2        // true
x < "12"      // true
x == "abc"    // false
x < "abc"     // false
x > "abc"     // false
y == ""       // true
y === ""      // false
z == true     // true
!z == false   // true
z == 1        // true
!z == 0       // true
z == y        // false
w == "cat"    // true
w == "cat "   // false (spaces count)
w == "Cat"    // false (comparisons are case-sensitive)
w > "Cat"     // true
w < "abc"     // false
```

Tip: Strict comparison operators (=== and !==) are found in JavaScript and PHP, but not in most C-style languages.

Precedence Rules

Recall from "Controlling Calculation Order" on page 29 that precedence determines the priority of various operators when more than one is used in an expression. Comparison operators have higher precedence than logical operators do. The expression:

```
x > y && a == 1
```

is equivalent to:

```
(x > y) && (a == 1)
```

and not to:

```
x > (y && a) == 1
```

You can combine multiple logical operators in a single expression. From highest to lowest priority, the operators are !, &&, and ||. For example, the expression:

```
x && !y || z
```

is equivalent to:

```
(x && (!y)) || z
```

Arithmetic operators (page 26) have higher precedence than comparison operators and logical operators do.

Control Flow Statements

We now have the basic pieces for writing conditional code: variables, values, data types, booleans, and operators.

When the JavaScript interpreter runs conditional code, it may execute statements in perfect sequence, skip statements, repeat others, or jump forward or back to still others. **Control flow** is the execution sequence of statements in your program, and you determine this flow with **control flow statements** (and with input data, but I'm not discussing that topic in this chapter). The control flow statements `if`, `switch`, `while`, and `for` use boolean conditions or iteration to determine whether the interpreter executes a series of statements.

- The `if` and `switch` statements are called **conditional statements** because they execute a block of code based on whether a specified condition prevails.

- The `while` and `for` statements are called **loops** or **iterative statements** because they repeat a block of code a specified number of times or until a particular condition becomes false.

The if Statement

Terminology

Parentheses	Braces	Brackets
()	{}	[]

The `if` statement, which is part of every programming language, executes statements if a condition is true. The syntax of the `if` statement in JavaScript (and other C-style languages) is:

```
if (condition)
  statement
```

condition is an expression that evaluates to true or false (that is, a boolean expression). *statement* is a statement that is executed if *condition* evaluates to true. For example, the condition x > 1 is true in the following program, so running this program executes the `alert` statement, which opens an alert box displaying the message "5 is greater than 1".

```
var x = 5;
if (x > 1)
  alert(x + " is greater than 1");
```

You can also write the `if` statement on one line:

```
if (x > 1) alert(x + " is greater than 1");
```

The `alert` statement in the following program isn't executed because the condition x == y is false.

```
var x = 5;
var y = 10;
if (x == y)
  alert(x + " is equal to " + y);
```

To execute multiple statements if *condition* is true, use the syntax:

```
if (condition) {
  block
}
```

block is a block statement. A **block statement** (or **compound statement**) is used to group zero or more statements delimited by a pair of curly braces. The interpreter treats the statements that comprise the block as a single unit.

```
{
  statement_1;
  statement_2;
  ...
  statement_n;
}
```

Tip: Parentheses, brackets, and braces are always used in pairs. If you have an opening one, then a closing one is required. It may be many lines later, but it must exist. See also "Brace Placement" on page 76.

The block statement in following program computes z and then opens an alert box displaying the value of z.

```
var x, y, z;
x = 5;
y = 10;
if (x > 1 && y != 0) {
  z = x / y;
  alert("z is equal to " + z);
}
```

If a condition contains multiple boolean expressions joined by logical operators, then you can make the code more readable by surrounding each expression with parentheses. For example, you can write the preceding if statement more clearly as:

```
if ((x > 1) && (y != 0)) {...
```

if-else

You can add an else clause to an if statement to execute a block of statements if the condition is false. The syntax is:

```
if (condition) {
  block1
} else {
  block2
}
```

condition is evaluated. If it's true, then *block1* is executed; otherwise, *block2* is executed.

The following program displays the message "8 is even".

```
var a = 8;
if (a % 2 == 0) {
  alert(a + " is even");
} else {
  alert(a + " is odd");
}
```

The following program displays the message "Can't divide by zero".

```
var x, y, z;
x = 5;
y = 0;
if (y != 0) {
  z = x / y;
  alert("z is equal to " + z);
} else {
  alert("Can't divide by zero");
}
```

You can nest an if statement in an if statement. Be sure to indent the statements and braces to make your meaning clear. The following program displays the message "The balance is positive", but not the message "The balance is large".

```
var balance = 500;
if (balance >= 0) {
  alert("The balance is positive");
  if (balance > 10000) {
    alert("The balance is large");
  }
} else {
  alert("The balance is negative");
}
```

Don't overnest. JavaScript can handle a thousand levels of nested code blocks, but nesting deeper than three levels makes code hard for humans to read and comprehend.

if-else if

You can add an arbitrary number of else if clauses to an if statement to test several independent conditions. A trailing else clause specifies code to execute if none of the preceding conditions is true. The syntax is:

```
if (condition1) {
  block1
} else if (condition2) {
  block2
...
} else if (conditionN) {
  blockN
} else {
  default_block
}
```

Each condition is evaluated in order. First, *condition1* is evaluated. If it's true, then *block1* is executed; otherwise, *condition2* is evaluated. If *condition2* is true, then *block2* is executed, and so on. If no conditions are true, then *default_block* is executed. When a block is executed, the rest of the if structure is ignored.

The following program displays the message "a is equal to b".

```
var a = 5;
var b = 5;
if (a > b) {
  alert("a is greater than b");
} else if (a == b) {
  alert("a is equal to b");
} else {
  alert("a is less than b");
}
```

The following program displays the message "grade = C".

```
var grade;
var testScore = 79;
if (testScore >= 90) {
  grade = "A";
} else if (testScore >= 80) {
  grade = "B";
} else if (testScore >= 70) {
  grade = "C";
} else if (testScore >= 60) {
  grade = "D";
} else {
  grade = "F";
}
alert("grade = " + grade);
```

The switch Statement

The switch statement provides a clean and readable alternative to creating a long series of else if tests. The switch statement evaluates an expression, matches that expression's value to a case clause, and then executes the statements associated with that case. The syntax is:

```
switch (expression) {
  case value1:
    // Statements executed when expression matches value1
    break;
  case value2:
    // Statements executed when expression matches value2
    break;
  ...
  case valueN:
    // Statements executed when expression matches valueN
    break;
  default:
    // Statements executed when no value matches expression
    break;
}
```

The switch statement first evaluates *expression*. It then looks for the first case clause whose *value* equals *expression* (using strict comparison, ===) and transfers control to that clause, executing the associated statements. (If multiple cases match *expression*, then the first matching case is selected.) If no matching case clause is found, then the program looks for the optional default clause and, if found, executes the associated statements. If no default clause is found, then the program continues execution at the statement following the switch statement.

The optional break statement associated with each case clause ensures that the program breaks out of the switch statement after the matched case is executed and continues execution at the statement following the switch statement. If break is omitted, then the program continues execution at the next case (or default) clause in the switch statement. If you forget a break, then the program will run the statements in the following case clause, regardless of whether that case clause's *value* equals *expression*.

The following program displays the message "disease = Gyrate atrophy".

```javascript
var disease;
var gene = "OAT";
switch(gene) {
  case "IDDM2":
    disease = "Diabetes";
    break;
  case "OAT":
    disease = "Gyrate atrophy";
    break;
  case "PAH":
    disease = "phenylketonuria";
    break;
  case "VMD2":
    disease = "Best disease";
    break;
  default:
    disease = "Unknown gene";
}
alert("disease = " + disease);
```

Sometimes you will want different cases to use the same block of statements. You can do so by omitting a break statement. If no break follows a case clause, then execution continues at ("falls through to") the next case clause regardless of its criteria. The following program displays the message "colorType = secondary".

```javascript
var colorType;
var color = "green";
switch(color) {
  case "red":
  case "blue":
  case "yellow":
    colorType = "primary";
    break;
  case "orange":
  case "green":
  case "purple":
    colorType = "secondary";
    break;
  default:
    colorType = "Unknown color";
}
alert("colorType = " + colorType);
```

The while Statement

The while statement repeats a block of statements as long as a condition remains true. The syntax is:

```
while (condition) {
  block
}
```

condition is evaluated. If it's true, then *block* is executed. When *block* execution completes, *condition* is reevaluated, and if it's still true, then *block* is executed again. This process repeats until *condition* becomes false; then the loop terminates.

The following while loop iterates as long as n is less than three.

```
var n = 0;
var x = 0;
while (n < 3) {
  n++;
  x += n;
  alert("n = " + n + ", x = " + x);
}
```

In each iteration, the loop increments n and then adds it to x. Therefore, n and x take on the following values:

- After the first pass, n = 1 and x = 1

- After the second pass, n = 2 and x = 3

- After the third pass, n = 3 and x = 6

After completing the third pass, the condition n < 3 is no longer true, so the loop terminates.

The following while loop calculates the factorial of n. The factorial, denoted by *n!*, is the result of multiplying the successive integers from 1 through *n*. $n! = n \times (n-1) \times (n-2) \times \cdots \times 1$. The result is $5! = 5 \times 4 \times 3 \times 2 \times 1 = 120$.

```
var n = 5;
var fact = 1;
while (n > 0) {
  fact *= n;
  n--;
}
alert(fact);   // 120
```

The following `while` loop prints the Fibonacci sequence up to n. The Fibonacci sequence is the sequence of numbers, 1, 1, 2, 3, 5, 8, 13,... in which each number is equal to the sum of the two preceding numbers.

```
var n = 25;
var a = 0;
var b = 1;
var temp;
while (b < n) {
  alert(b);  // 1 1 2 3 5 8 13 21
  temp = b;
  b = a + b;
  a = temp;
}
```

Infinite Loops

A loop condition that remains true permanently causes an **infinite loop** (or **endless loop**). In the following program, for example, I want to print the squares of the odd integers from 9 down to 0. But the program enters an infinite loop because the value of n jumps from 1 to –1 and never *equals* zero, which would make the condition n != 0 false and halt the loop. To fix this problem, change the loop condition to n >= 0.

```
var n = 9;
while (n != 0) {     // Always true!
  alert("n = " + n + ", n * n = " + n * n);
  n -= 2;
}
```

The output is:

```
n = 9, n * n = 81
n = 7, n * n = 49
n = 5, n * n = 25
n = 3, n * n = 9
n = 1, n * n = 1
n = -1, n * n = 1
n = -3, n * n = 9
...                 // Infinite loop - program runs forever
```

To break out of an infinite loop, close the browser tab in which the program is running. You might have to first select the checkbox that prevents the tab from creating additional dialog boxes. In other languages, you might have to press a keyboard shortcut (like Ctrl+Z) to kill a program.

To avoid creating an infinite loop in your programs, make sure that a statement in the loop's code block modifies a value in the condition in a way that will eventually make the condition false. It's provably impossible to write a procedure that can determine whether a program has entered an infinite loop (in case you're considering doing so).

The do Statement

A less frequently used variation of the `while` loop is the `do` loop, which executes its code block at least once before checking whether the condition is true. It then repeats the loop until the condition is false. The syntax is:

```
do {
  block
} while (condition);
```

The following do loop iterates at least once and then reiterates until i is no longer less than 5.

```
var i = 0;
do {
  alert(i);
  i++;
} while (i < 5);
```

The for Statement

After you write a few `while` loops, you'll notice a common three-part pattern emerge:

- Set up a counter to keep track of the loop (this counter is declared and initialized before the loop itself)

- Check the condition

- Update (increment or decrement) the counter inside the loop, typically at the end of the loop

In a program, these three pieces look like this:

```
var i = 1;            // Set up the loop counter
while (i < 10) {      // Check the condition
  // do stuff
  // do stuff
  // ...
  i++                 // Update the counter
}
```

The `for` statement, which iterates over a sequence of values, brings these three pieces together in a single, easy-to-read statement. The following `for` loop is equivalent to the preceding `while` loop.

```
for (var i = 1; i < 10; i++) {
  // do stuff
  // do stuff
  // ...
}
```

The syntax is:

```
for (initialize; condition; update) {
  block
}
```

initialize can be any expression but is typically used to initialize (and optionally declare with var) a counter variable. *initialize* is executed only once, as the loop (code block) starts. *condition* is evaluated before each loop iteration. If *condition* is true, then *block* is executed; otherwise, the loop terminates. *update* is evaluated at the end of each loop iteration, before the next evaluation of *condition*, and is typically used to update (increment or decrement) the counter variable.

Tip: The variables i, j, and k are often used as loop counters.

The following for loop prints the numbers 0, 1, . . . , 4. It declares the counter variable i and initializes it to zero. The condition checks whether i is less than 5. And i is incremented by one after each pass through the loop.

```
for (var i = 0; i < 5; i++) {
  alert(i);
}
```

You can initialize multiple counters or variables, separated by commas, in the loop header. The following for loop calculates the factorial of n and is equivalent to the while loop on page 46.

```
for (var n = 5, fact = 1; n > 0; n--) {
  fact *= n;
}
alert(fact);  // 120
```

The following nested for loops print a multiplication table.

```
for (var i = 1; i <= 5; i++) {
  for (var j = 1; j <= 5; j++) {
    alert("i = " + i + ", j = " + j + ", i * j = " + i * j);
  }
}
```

The output is:

```
i = 1, j = 1, i * j = 1
i = 1, j = 2, i * j = 2
i = 1, j = 3, i * j = 3
...     // Lines omitted for brevity
i = 5, j = 4, i * j = 20
i = 5, j = 5, i * j = 25
```

More About for

These examples demonstrate simple uses of for statements. Each of the three expressions in the loop header can actually be any type of expression. *initialize* doesn't have to set up a counter, for example, nor must *update* increment or decrement a counter. JavaScript doesn't care—it simply evaluates the specified expressions at the appropriate times as it cycles through the loop. You can even omit any expression (for(;;) is a valid loop header), provided that loop-control statements are specified elsewhere before or during the loop. Experienced programmers (particularly C programmers) often find creative and compact ways to use for loops.

Skipping Part of a Loop Iteration

By default, all statements in a loop block are executed during each iteration. You can use a continue statement in the body of a while or for loop to skip part of an iteration if a given condition is true. In the block of a while or for loop, type:

```
if (condition) {
  statements
  continue;
}
```

You can include optional *statements* to execute before the continue. When the interpreter encounters continue, it skips the rest of the statements in the loop, jumps back to the top of a loop, and goes back to either testing the loop condition (in a while loop) or continuing with the next counter value (in a for loop).

The following for loop uses continue to print the squares of the even integers between 0 and 10, inclusive.

```
for (var i = 0, sq; i <= 10; i++) {
  if (i % 2 != 0) {
    continue;
  }
  sq = i * i;
  alert("i = " + i + ", i * i = " + sq);
}
```

The output is:

```
i = 0, i * i = 0
i = 2, i * i = 4
i = 4, i * i = 16
i = 6, i * i = 36
i = 8, i * i = 64
i = 10, i * i = 100
```

Tip: If a loop containing continue is nested in another loop, then continue jumps to the top of the inner loop, not the outer one.

Exiting a Loop

By default, all statements in a loop block are executed during each iteration. You can use a break statement in the body of a while or for loop to jump out of a loop if a given condition is true. In the block of a while or for loop, type:

```
if (condition) {
  statements
  break;
}
```

You can include optional *statements* to execute before the break. When the interpreter encounters break, it terminates the loop.

The following for loop prints the square roots of a decreasing series of integers (4, 3, 2,...). It uses break to exit the loop at the first negative number that it encounters.

```
for (var i = 4; i >= -4; i--) {
  if (i < 0) {
    break;
  }
  alert("i = " + i + ", sqrt(i) = " + Math.sqrt(i));
}
```

The output is:

```
i = 4, sqrt(i) = 2
i = 3, sqrt(i) = 1.7320508075688772
i = 2, sqrt(i) = 1.4142135623730951
i = 1, sqrt(i) = 1
i = 0, sqrt(i) = 0
```

Tip: If a loop containing **break** is nested in another loop, then **break** terminates the inner loop but not the outer one.

CHAPTER 5

Functions

JavaScript, like all programming languages, lets you create your own functions. You've already seen a few of JavaScript's built-in functions: the alert() and prompt() functions were used in the first programs that we wrote. Functions provide several benefits:

- They make programs modular and manageable

- They encapsulate computations and separate the high-level logic from the details

- They're reusable and allow you to perform a well-defined task multiple times in multiple places with various initial values

Functions have different names in different languages. They're also called modules, subroutines, subprograms, routines, or methods.

Creating a Function

A **function** is a named block of statements that performs an operation. The `function` statement creates a new function and defines its name, parameters, and the block of statements that it executes when it's called. The syntax is:

```
function functionName(paramList) {
    block
}
```

functionName is the unique name of the function, *paramList* represents zero or more comma-separated parameters (described later in this chapter), and *block* is a block of statements that comprise the body of the function.

The following `function` statements define three simple functions. The aptly named `doNothing()` function is the simplest possible JavaScript function. `printMessage()` prints the string "Hello, world!". `isEven()` has a parameter list; it prints "true" if its argument is an even number, or "false" otherwise.

```
function doNothing() {
}
```

```
function printMessage() {
    alert("Hello, world!");
}
```

```
function isEven(num) {
    alert(num % 2 == 0);
}
```

Calling a Function

Functions don't run when they're defined; you must invoke them explicitly. A **function call** is an expression that executes a function. The part of a program from which a function is called is termed the **caller**. You've already seen calls to JavaScript's built-in functions throughout this book (`alert("Hello")`, for example). User-defined functions are called in the same way: by using the name of the function followed by a parenthesized list of arguments. The syntax is:

```
functionName(argumentList)
```

argumentList represents zero or more comma-separated arguments that are passed to the function. Even if you're not passing a function any arguments, you still must include empty parentheses in the function call. When a function is executed, the caller stops until the function finishes running, and then control returns to the caller. Pass arguments to a function in the exact order in which the parameters are given in the function definition.

The following function calls invoke the three functions defined above:

```
doNothing();
printMessage();
isEven(6);
```

The doNothing() function produces no output. The printMessage() function opens an alert box with the message "Hello, world!". The isEven() function opens an alert box with the message "true" (because 6 is an even number).

Returning a Value from a Function

A **return value** is the result of a function that is sent back to the caller of the function. You can specify a return value by using a return statement in the body of the function. The syntax is:

```
return expression;
```

The return statement ends the current function call. It evaluates *expression* and sends it back to the caller as the return value. If *expression* is omitted, then it defaults to undefined.

The syntax to store the returned value of a function in a variable is:

```
variable = functionName(argumentList);
```

When executed, the caller stops until the function finishes running, and then control returns to the caller. The function's return value is assigned to *variable*.

The following function returns the square of its argument.

```
function square(x) {
  return x * x;
}
```

Here are some example function calls to square():

```
var a, sq1, sq2, sq3;
a = 5;
sq1 = square(a);
sq2 = square(-2.5);
sq3 = square(square(2));
alert("sq1 = " + sq1 + ", sq2 = " + sq2 + ", sq3 = " + sq3);
```

The output is:

```
sq1 = 25, sq2 = 6.25, sq3 = 16
```

Note that you can use a function call as an argument in a function call, provided the nested function returns a compatible value. The expression square(square(2)) resolves to square(4). You can also use JavaScript's built-in functions and methods as arguments: square(Math.max(-4, 2, 0)).

Parameters Aren't Arguments

Sometimes you might see the terms *parameter* and *argument* used interchangeably, but they differ. A **parameter** is a name in the parameter list of a function definition's header (the function statement). It receives a value from the caller of the function. An **argument** is the actual value or reference passed to a function by the caller.

In this function definition, for example, x and y are parameters:

```
function sum(x, y) {
  return x + y;
}
```

And in this function call, 2 and 3 * 5 are arguments:

```
z = sum(2, 3 * 5);
```

When you write a function that returns a value, keep in mind that when the JavaScript interpreter executes a return statement, it immediately jumps out of the function and back to the caller. The var statement in the following function, for example, will never be executed.

```
function add2(x, y) {
  return x + y;
  var message = "hello";
}
```

In this situation, the interpreter might warn you with a message like "unreachable code after return statement". The return statement is usually the last line of a function, although occasionally you may want to specify a condition to leave a function early.

The following function returns the range of three numbers. The range is difference between the lowest and highest values.

```
function range(x, y, z) {
  return Math.max(x, y, z) - Math.min(x, y, z);
}
```

The function call range(5, 2, 9) returns the value 7.

The following function determines whether its argument is a prime number and returns true or false. A prime number is an integer greater than one that has no positive divisors other than one and itself. Note that isPrime() has two return statements; control returns to the caller when either statement is encountered.

```
function isPrime(n) {
  var divisor = Math.floor(n / 2);    // Initial divisor
  while (divisor > 1) {
    if (n % divisor == 0)
      return false;
    divisor--;
  }
  return true;
}
```

The following for loop determines whether the integers from 2 to 10 are prime.

```
for (var i = 2; i <= 10; i++) {
  if (isPrime(i))
    alert(i + " is prime.")
  else
    alert(i + " is not prime.");
}
```

The output is:

```
2 is prime.
3 is prime.
4 is not prime.
5 is prime.
6 is not prime.
7 is prime.
8 is not prime.
9 is not prime.
10 is not prime.
```

Tip: If control flows off the end of a function without encountering a **return** statement, then **undefined** is returned.

Variable Scope

When you declare a variable inside a function, only code within that function can read or change the variable's value because its scope is **local** to that function. All variables in the function's parameter list are also local variables.

In the following function, the variable x is local to the printSum() function. When printSum() terminates, x is destroyed. a and b are also destroyed when printSum() terminates.

```
function printSum(a, b) {
  var x = a + b;    // x is local to printSum()
  alert(x);
}
```

Trying to use x outside printSum() causes an error:

```
printSum(2, 3);    // OK: Sets local x equal to 5
var y = x * 2;     // Error: x is undefined
```

A variable's **scope** defines the extent to which it can be referenced within a block of code. Scope can be local or global. A **global** variable declared outside a function can be accessed and changed by any function.

In the following code, the variable x is global because it's declared outside a function. When you use x (or any global variable) inside a function, make sure not to redeclare it with a var statement—you want the function to look for global variables outside its local scope.

```
var x;    // x is a global variable

function printSum(a, b) {
  x = a + b;    // Use an assignment, not a var statement
  alert(x);
}
```

The global variable x is available inside and outside printSum():

```
printSum(2, 3);    // OK: Sets global x equal to 5
var y = x * 2;     // OK: Sets y equal to 10
```

Undeclared variables are always global. If you assign a value to a variable that hasn't been declared with var, then it become a global variable automatically. Don't create global variables unless you intend to.

```
function myFunction() {
  myVar = "I'm undeclared, so I'm global";
}

myFunction();    // Creates global myVar (intentionally?)
alert(myVar)     // OK(?): prints myVar
```

Use Globals Sparingly

Every language has its own rules that govern the scope and lifetime of variables and determine how naming conflicts are resolved for differently scoped variables. In Java, for example, a pair of braces {...} generally defines a particular scope. If you declare the loop counter variable i in a for loop header, then i is local to only that loop and can't be accessed outside it.

Be cautious about where you declare variables and where they can be read or changed. Although broadly scoped variables are useful in some situations, overuse of globals frequently leads to messy dependencies and protracted debugging sessions. You should communicate with functions via arguments and return values.

Before the JavaScript interpreter
runs a program, it first scans
(parses) all the code to determine which functions exist.
Consequently, it doesn't matter where you define functions
or how you order them in a JavaScript (.js) file. You can call
a function and then define it,
or vice versa. The best practice,
however, is to define all functions at the top of the JavaScript
file, before they're called. This
practice organizes code in a
consistent and readable format.
In some other languages, you
must define or declare functions
before calling them.

Splitting Code Into Different Files

Programs can grow quickly to hundreds or thousands of lines of code,
making them difficult to read and navigate even though they're split into
functions. To make your code more manageable, put groups of related
functions in different files rather than storing all the code in a single file.
Grouping functions into different files also makes it easier for several people
to work on the same project by working on separate files. In complex applications built by teams of software developers, it's not unusual to have
hundreds or thousands of separate code files for one project. Web developers don't normally split JavaScript code into hundreds of files, however—a
handful of files usually suffices.

You can use HTML <script> tags to tell a webpage where to find
JavaScript files. If you've been following along by using the example files
(page 2), then you've been using the <script> tag all along in the file
run.html (see "Up and Running with JavaScript" on page 13.) After
you split your JavaScript code into multiple files, simply add a <script>
tag for each file. The browser's built-in JavaScript interpreter loads the
specified files and runs the code inside them. The following HTML code
links to the three JavaScript files named script1.js, script2.js, and script3.js:

```
<html>
  <head>
    <title>Webpage Title</title>
  </head>
  <body>
    <div>
      <p>Webpage content...</p>
    </div>
    <script src="script1.js"></script>
    <script src="script2.js"></script>
    <script src="script3.js"></script>
  </body>
</html>
```

The order of <script> tags is important because the interpreter runs
the code in the order that the files are listed. If script3.js contains functions
that are called by code in script1.js, then load script3.js before script1.js:

```
<script src="script3.js"></script>
<script src="script1.js"></script>
<script src="script2.js"></script>
```

When you move your code into different files in JavaScript (or any
language), keep track of cross-file dependencies and the order in which
files will need to be loaded. Load important and widely used functions
first. (Having said that, it's perfectly acceptable to keep the short programs
in this book in one script file.)

CHAPTER 6

More About Strings

R ecall from "Working with Strings" on page 33 that a string is a sequence of zero of more characters surrounded by double or single quotes:

```
"This is a string."
```

```
'So is this.'
```

String variables are more than just places to hold characters, however. In JavaScript and other modern programming languages, you can use string-related properties and methods to inspect and manipulate strings. A property is a built-in attribute of an object. Length (number of characters) is a property of a string, for example. A method works like a function, but is associated with a specific type of object. You can use string-related methods to change the case of a string, extract certain characters from a string, and so on. (Objects are covered in Chapter 11, but you don't need to know the details yet.)

The . (dot) operator is used to access properties and methods:

```
var str = "This is a string.";
var len = str.length;        // 17
var up = str.toUpperCase();  // "THIS IS A STRING."
```

This chapter covers JavaScript's commonly used string properties and methods.

Numbers Stored as Strings

There's a big difference between:

```
var x = 123;
```

and:

```
var y = "123";
```

The value of x is the number 123 and the value of y is the string "123"—not the number 123, but the characters 1, 2, and 3. JavaScript treats actual numbers differently from strings that look like numbers.

Store numbers as strings if those numbers aren't involved in arithmetic calculations. Store telephone numbers, credit-card numbers, postal codes, and government and employee ID numbers as strings, for example. This technique can save space and prevent data loss: if you store the postal code "02116" as a number instead of as a string, then you'll lose the leading zero. Or worse: some JavaScript interpreters treat numbers that have leading zeros as octal (base 8) numbers.

Numbers stored as strings are compared lexicographically, not arithmetically. The string "2" is greater than the string "12", for example, because (alphabetically) "1" precedes "2". So, the condition "2" < "12" is false and "2" > "12" is true.

Finding the Length of a String

The length property counts the number of characters in a string. length counts everything in the string: letters, digits, punctuation, whitespace, symbols, escape characters, and so on. An escape character (page 34) looks like more than one character but represents only one. A string with no characters ("" or '') is called an **empty string** or **null string**.

```
var str1 = "This is a string.";
var str2 = "12345";
var str3 = " ";              // Space character
var str4 = "";               // Empty string
var str5 = "\n";             // Escape character
var str6 = "\"Hello\"";      // Escape characters

var len1 = str1.length;      // 17
var len2 = str2.length;      // 5
var len3 = str3.length;      // 1
var len4 = str4.length;      // 0
var len5 = str5.length;      // 1
var len6 = str6.length;      // 7
```

Concatenating Strings

Use the + (concatenation) operator to combine, or concatenate, strings. Concatenation joins two strings into a single string. Concatenation doesn't add a space between strings.

```
var str1 = "Hello";
var str2 = "world";
var str3 = "abc";
var str4 = " ";              // Space character
var str5 = "";               // Empty string
var str6 = "Don\'t.";        // Escape character

var concat1 = str1 + str2            // Helloworld
var concat2 = str1 + ", " + str2;    // Hello, world
var concat3 = str3 + str4 + str3;    // abc abc
var concat4 = str3 + str5 + str3;    // abcabc
var concat5 = str5 + str5 + str5;    // Empty string
var concat6 = "\"" + str6 + "\"";    // "Don't." (with quotes)
```

You can also concatenate strings by using the += assignment operator (page 32).

```
var str7 = "aaa";
var str8 = "bbb";
str7 += str8;      // aaabbb
str7 += "ccc";     // aaabbbccc
```

If the two operands are a string and a number (page 25), then JavaScript automatically converts the number to a string before concatenating.

```
var strTwo = "2";
var numTwo = 2;
var concat7 = numTwo + numTwo;   // 4  (a number)
var concat8 = strTwo + strTwo;   // 22 (a string)
var concat9 = strTwo + numTwo;   // 22 (a string)
```

If the two operands are a string and a boolean (page 35), then JavaScript automatically converts the boolean to "true" or "false" before concatenating.

```
var str9 = "It's ";
var boolTrue = true;
var boolFalse = false;
var concat10 = str9 + boolTrue;    // It's true  (a string)
var concat11 = str9 + boolFalse;   // It's false (a string)
```

Tip: Automatic type conversions also apply to comparison operators (page 38).

You can also use the concat() method to combine one or more strings. The syntax is:

```
str.concat(string1, string2, ..., stringN)
```

This method doesn't change the original string (*str*).

```
var s1 = "Hello";
var s2 = "world";
var greeting = s1.concat(", ", s2, "!");    // Hello, world!
```

Tip: Favor the + and += operators, which are more efficient than the concat() method.

Operator Overloading

Recall that the + and += operators are also used to add two numbers. Using + and += for both addition and string concatenation is an example of **operator overloading**, which is the assignment of more than one function to a particular operator. The operation performed depends on the data types of the operands involved. Here, + and += behave differently with numbers than they do with strings.

Changing String Case

The toLowerCase() and toUpperCase() methods change the case of a string. A **cased** character is a letter, which can be lowercase (*a*) or uppercase (*A*). Case changes affect only letters; digits, punctuation, whitespace, and escape characters are left unchanged. You can use these methods to format printed output or make case-insensitive comparisons (page 63). These methods don't change the original string.

```
var play = "King Lear";
var lower = play.toLowerCase();    // king lear
var upper = play.toUpperCase();    // KING LEAR
```

Trimming a String

The `trim()` method trims a string. Trimming strips extraneous whitespace from the beginning and end of a string (but doesn't remove whitespace from *within* a string). You can use `trim()` to clean up user-entered values or to trim strings before comparing them. Whitespace includes spaces and nonbreaking spaces, as well as the escape characters tab (\t), new line (\n), carriage return (\r), and form feed (\f). This method doesn't change the original string.

```
var str1 = "   John Q. Public   ";
var str2 = "\t   aaa      bbb  \n";    // Escape characters
var t1 = "|" + str1.trim() + "|";      // |John Q. Public|
var t2 = "|" + str2.trim() + "|";      // |aaa      bbb|
```

Repeating a String

The `repeat(count)` method repeats a string *count* (≥ 0) times. If *count* is zero, then an empty string is returned. If *count* isn't an integer, then it's truncated to an integer (3.8 is truncated to 3, for example). Repetition doesn't add a space between the strings and is more efficient than multiple concatenations (page 60). This method doesn't change the original string.

```
var str = "toyboat ";
var r0 = str.repeat(0);      // Empty string
var r1 = str.repeat(1);      // toyboat
var r2 = str.repeat(2.6);    // toyboat toyboat
var r3 = str.repeat(3);      // toyboat toyboat toyboat
```

Converting a String to a Number

A **NaN** (Not-a-Number) value results when you create an undefined or unrepresentable number. For example, the following expressions result in NaNs.

```
Math.sqrt(-1)
```

```
Math.log(-1)
```

```
10 / "A"
```

```
0 / 0
```

JavaScript has built-in functions that let you convert and test numbers and NaN values. The `Number(value)` function tries to convert *value* to a number and then returns the numeric value of *value* if successful, or NaN otherwise. The `isNaN(testValue)` function returns `true` if *testValue* is NaN or `undefined`, or `false` otherwise.

```
var foo = "45";     // May or may not be a number
var myNum = Number(foo);
if (isNaN(myNum))
  alert("It's not a number.")
else
  alert("It's a number.");
```

Usually, you're interested in whether a value *is* a number. JavaScript has no isNumber() function; instead, use the ! (not) operator to negate isNaN():

```
if (!isNaN(myNum)) {
  // It's a number
}
```

You can use these functions to check the validity of user-entered values. For example, you can determine whether a user entered a number in the "Age" field on a form.

Comparing Strings

You can compare strings by using the comparison operators (==, ===, !=, !==, <, <=, >, and >=), introduced in "Comparison Operators" on page 38. A comparison returns the boolean value true or false. JavaScript compares strings by evaluating the lexicographical ordering of their characters. To determine whether one string is equal to another, JavaScript first compares their initial characters. If those characters differ, JavaScript determines the truth of the comparison; otherwise, it compares the second characters, and so on.

Comparisons are case-sensitive. All uppercase letters are less than (precede) all lowercase letters, so *ABCD...* is less than *abcd....* The result of this logic is that "apple" precedes "bed" (as expected) but "Bed" precedes "apple" (unlike a dictionary). To do a case-insensitive comparison, convert the strings to lowercase or uppercase (page 61).

```
"Cat" == "cat"          // false
"cat" == "cat" + ""     // true
"cat" <= "cat"          // true
"CAT" != "CAT "         // true
"A" < "a"               // true
"A" < "AA"              // true
"A" < ""                // false
"abc" > "abcd"          // false
"able" < "baker"        // true
"Baker" < "able"        // true
"isRed" < "isred"       // true
"is red" < "is_red"     // true
"is_red" < "isred"      // true
"ABC".toLowerCase() == "abc".toLowerCase()     // true
```

Dividing zero by zero returns NaN, but dividing a nonzero number by zero doesn't return NaN, as you might expect. An arithmetic operation the returns a number that exceeds the limit of a floating-point number returns Infinity (positive infinity) or -Infinity (negative infinity). These values behave mathematically like infinity.

```
1/0             // Infinity
-1/0            // -Infinity
Infinity + 1    // Infinity
Math.pow(10, 1000)
                // Infinity
Math.log(0)     // -Infinity
1 / Infinity    // 0
```

To determine whether a value is infinite, compare it (==, !=) to Number.POSITIVE_INFINITY or Number.NEGATIVE_INFINITY. Or use the built-in function Number.isFinite(*value*), which returns true if *value* is infinite or NaN, or false otherwise.

Extracting Characters from a String

A string is an ordered sequence of characters. An individual character is identified by its position, or **index**, in the sequence. JavaScript, like most languages, uses zero-based indexes: the first character is at index zero, the second is at index one, and so on. The index of the last character is the length of the string minus one (*str*.length - 1).

The charAt(*index*) method returns the specified character of a string. *index* is an integer between zero and one less than the length of the string. If *index* is omitted, then it defaults to zero. If *index* is out of range, then an empty string is returned. If *index* isn't an integer, then it's truncated to an integer (3.8 is truncated to 3, for example).

```
var str = "Hello, world!";
var ch1 = str.charAt(0);                // H
var ch2 = str.charAt(1);                // e
var ch3 = str.charAt(str.length - 1);   // !
var ch4 = str.charAt();                 // H
var ch5 = str.charAt(100);              // Empty string
```

A **slice** is a substring of a string specified by two indexes that demarcate a sequence of contiguous characters. The slice(*beginSlice, endSlice*) method returns the specified slice from a string. Slicing returns the substring starting with the first index and up but not including the second index. If *endSlice* is omitted, then the returned slice contains the characters from *beginSlice* to the end of the string. A negative index counts from the end of the string.

```
var str = "sequoia";
var slice1 = str.slice(0);        // sequoia
var slice2 = str.slice(3);        // uoia
var slice3 = str.slice(2, 5);     // quo
var slice4 = str.slice(2, -2);    // quo
var slice5 = str.slice(-1);       // a
var slice6 = str.slice(-3);       // oia
var slice7 = str.slice(-3, -1);   // oi
var slice8 = str.slice(0, -1);    // sequoi
```

Tip: The substr() and substring() methods also return a substring of a string. I prefer slice(), but you can explore those other methods if you like.

Searching for Substrings

JavaScript's various search methods find substrings in strings. These methods take an optional argument that restricts the search area, which is useful for finding a substring beyond its initial occurrence. String indexes are zero-based: the first character is at index zero, the second is at index one, and so on. All searches are case-sensitive; to do a case-insensitive search, convert the strings to lowercase or uppercase (page 61).

The indexOf(*searchValue, start*) method returns the position of the first occurrence of *searchValue* in a string, starting the search at *start*. If *start* is omitted, then the entire string is searched. If *searchValue* is not found, then –1 is returned.

```
var str = "Peter the pepper eater";
var idx1 = str.indexOf("er");          // 3
var idx2 = str.indexOf("er", 5);       // 14
var idx3 = str.indexOf("er", 17);      // 20
var idx4 = str.indexOf("the", 0);      // 6
var idx5 = str.indexOf("the", 6);      // 6
var idx6 = str.indexOf("");            // 0
var idx7 = str.indexOf("", 8);         // 8
var idx8 = str.indexOf("Peter");       // 0
var idx9 = str.indexOf("peter");       // -1 (case-sensitive)
var idx10 = str.indexOf("Peter", 2);   // -1
```

The following program prints the message "The word does not occur."

```
var word = "fabric";
var quote = "I have nothing in common with myself.";
if (quote.indexOf(word) == -1) {
  alert("The word does not occur.");
}
```

The lastIndexOf(*searchValue, start*) method works like indexOf() but returns the position the final occurrence of *searchValue* in the string, which might be useful if you're working with large amounts of text.

```
var str = "Peter the pepper eater";
var last = str.lastIndexOf("er");     // 20
```

Other related methods include startsWith(*searchValue, start*), endsWith(*searchValue, start*), includes(*searchValue, start*), search(*searchValue*), and replace(*searchValue, newValue*).

You don't have to memorize all this information. The important thing here is to understand that JavaScript, like all modern programming languages, provides many ways to inspect and manipulate strings. You can always look up the syntax in a reference guide and find cookbooks and examples online.

Using Regular Expressions

Often we're interested in the format of a string rather than its literal value. You might want to determine whether a user-entered string is an email address, for example—not a specific email address but a string that matches the pattern of a valid email address. Similarly, you might want to determine whether a string is a valid URL. Or whether a password is a mixture of uppercase letters, lowercase letters, and special symbols. Or whether a credit-card number or a telephone number has the correct number of digits.

A **regular expression** is a sequence of characters that forms a pattern. You can use this pattern to match text in strings. Regular expressions are built into many programming languages, including JavaScript. They take practice to use correctly, but they're quite useful. In JavaScript, you can construct a regular expression in two ways. A regular expression literal consists of a pattern enclosed by slashes:

```
/pattern/
```

For example:

```
var myRE = /hello/;
```

Alternatively, you can call the RegExp() function with the keyword new:

```
new RegExp(pattern)
```

For example:

```
var myRE = new RegExp("hello");
```

Either way, you're creating a new regular expression object. JavaScript is what's called an object-oriented language, and the word new in the second example is what actually creates an object. Objects are covered in Chapter 11.

You can use the test(str) method to determine whether a regular expression pattern occurs in a specified string. This method returns true if a match exists, or false otherwise.

The following program prints the message "Found a match."

```
var myRE = /with/;
var quote = "I have nothing in common with myself.";
if (myRE.test(quote)) {
  alert("Found a match.");
}
```

Regular expression objects have methods in addition to test() that match, search, and replace text. You can also use regular expressions as arguments in some string methods, including match(regExp), search(regExp), and replace(regExp, newValue).

Simple patterns like /hello/ and /with/ are used to find direct matches. The pattern /abc/, for example, matches character combinations in strings in which the characters "abc" appear together, in order. A match would occur in the strings "Do you know your abc's?" and "A dabchick is a small water bird." No match would occur in the string "Lab chemical" because of the space character between "ab" and "c".

When a search requires a more-complex match, such as finding one or more b's or finding whitespace, then the pattern includes special characters. The pattern /ab*c/, for example, matches any character combination in which "a" is followed by zero or more "b"s (a * means zero or more occurrences of the preceding item) and is then followed immediately by "c". In the string "acbbabbbcde", the pattern /ab*c/ matches the substrings "ac" and "abbbc". The following table gives more examples of patterns that use special characters.

Special characters used in regular expressions

Pattern	Description
/^abc/	The ^ (caret) matches the beginning of a string. /^abc/ matches "abcdef" but not "defabc".
/abc$/	The $ matches the end of a string. /abc$/ matches "defabc" but not "abcdef".
/ab+c/	The + matches the preceding expression one or more times. /ab+c/ matches "abc" and "abbbc", but not "ac".
/ab*c/	The * matches the preceding expression zero or more times. /ab*c/ matches "ac", "abc", and "abbbc".
/ab?c/	The ? matches the preceding expression zero or one times. /ab?c/ matches "ac" and "abc", but not "abbc".
/abc|def/	The | (pipe) matches the expression on either side of the |. /green|yellow/ matches "green banana" and "yellow banana".
/a.c/	The . (dot) matches any single character. /.re./ matches "Tree", "area", and "fret".
/\bcat/	The \b matches a word boundary (the start or end of a word), such as a space or a new line.
/[bdfj]og/	Square brackets match any one of the characters in the brackets. /[bdfj]og/ matches "bog", "dog", "fog", and "jog", but not "log".

The preceding table lists only a few special characters. Many more are available, and you can combine them to create complex patterns. The following pattern, for example, matches a United States five-digit zip (postal) code with an optional four-digit extension.

```
/^[0-9]{5}(?:-[0-9]{4})?$/
```

Almost everyone starts out using regular expressions by looking for examples online. There's no need to create patterns from scratch for postal codes, dates, telephone numbers, credit-card numbers, IP addresses, URLs, HTML tags, user names, passwords, and other common patterns. The following pattern matches an email address.

```
/^[a-zA-Z0-9._%+-]+@[a-zA-Z0-9.-]+\.[a-zA-Z]{2,4}$/
```

Email addresses are notoriously difficult to match because they follow many complex rules. The pattern for a valid email address encompasses much more than matching the familiar *someone@domain.com*. In fact, the perfect regular expression for an email address is a bit of a holy grail for regular expression gurus. The pattern above looks complex, but you can simplify it by breaking it into its repetitive parts. It's not perfect, but it's the type of example you'll find online. Often you'll find patterns that are imperfect but adequate for what you're trying to match.

When you're new to regular expressions, focus on what they can be used for and how to implement them in your chosen programming language. You might never need to memorize their syntax—plenty of programmers get by just fine by copying and pasting regular expressions that they find online.

CHAPTER 7

Arrays

Parentheses	Braces	Brackets
()	{}	[]

Arrays, like strings, are ordered sequences of items. But whereas strings hold only characters, arrays hold collections of arbitrary items. Arrays can contain any items of any type (including other arrays); can grow and shrink as needed; and are easy to sort, search, and modify. Arrays are enclosed in brackets, as follows:

```
[1, "hello", -12.34, true]
```

In practice, arrays are typically used to store related items, ordered series, sequences of dates or integers, or attributes of the same entity.

```
["hearts", "diamonds", "clubs", "spades"]
```

```
["Mon", "Tue", "Wed", "Thu", "Fri", "Sat", "Sun"]
```

```
[1950, 1960, 1970, 1980, 1990, 2000, 2010, 2020]
```

```
["John", "Smith", 1972, "Male", "Los Angeles", "CA", "US"]
```

A benefit of arrays is that they store multiple values in a single named variable. You can use an array to store the names of every country, for example, instead of creating hundreds of variables:

```
var countries = ["Afghanistan", "Akrotiri", ..., "Zimbabwe"];
```

You can use array-related properties and methods to inspect and manipulate arrays. Length (number of items) is a property of an array, for example. You can use array-related methods to add or delete array items, sort array items, and so on. The . (dot) operator is used to access properties and methods (countries.length or countries.sort(), for example). Properties and methods are discussed in more detail in Chapter 11.

Creating an Array

Creating an array is straightforward: simply enclose zero or more comma-separated values in brackets. Each item in an array is called an **element**. An **empty array** contains no elements.

```
var empty = [];
var primes = [2, 3, 5, 7, 11, 13, 17, 19];
var operators = ["+", "-", "*", "/", "%"];
var parks = ["Yosemite", "Yellowstone", "Grand Canyon"];
```

Spaces and line breaks are ignored. An array declaration can span multiple lines:

```
var parks = [
  "Yosemite",
  "Yellowstone",
  "Grand Canyon"
];
```

Tip: Never put a comma after the last element (like `"Grand Canyon",`). The effect is inconsistent across browsers.

You can specify array elements by using expressions, which the interpreter evaluates when it creates the array.

```
var num = 2;
var str1 = "Hello";
var str2 = "world!";
var bool = true;
var myArray = [num + 1, Math.PI, str1 + ", " + str2, !bool];
```

The resulting array is:

```
[3, 3.141592653589793, "Hello, world!", false]
```

Finding the Length of an Array

The `length` property counts the number of elements in an array.

```
var len1 = empty.length;        // 0
var len2 = primes.length;       // 8
var len3 = operators.length;    // 5
var len4 = parks.length;        // 3
var len5 = myArray.length;      // 4
```

Indexing an Array

An array is an ordered sequence of elements. An individual element is identified by its position, or **index**, in the sequence. JavaScript, like most languages, uses zero-based indexes: the first element is at index zero, the second is at index one, and so on. The index of the last element is the length of the array minus one (*array*.length - 1).

The expression *array*[*index*] returns the specified element of an array. *index* is an integer between zero and one less than the length of the array. If *index* is out of range or isn't an integer, then undefined is returned.

```
var i = 2;
var item1 = primes[0];              // 2
var item2 = operators[i];           // *
var item3 = operators[i + 1];       // /
var item4 = parks[parks.length - 1]; // Grand Canyon
var item5 = parks[-1];              // undefined
var item6 = parks[5];               // undefined
var item7 = parks[1.0];             // Yellowstone
```

Looping Through an Array

You can think of an array more generally as a collection of items. Consider all the places that collections appear on your computer: the file system is a collection of files and folders, your email program is a collection of messages, your address book is a collection of contacts, and your music library is a collection of albums and playlists, each one being a collection of tracks. Collections appear everywhere in programming, and an array is the most straightforward and easy-to-understand type of collection.

You can iterate through the elements of an array by using a while loop or a for loop (Chapter 4). The following while loop prints all the elements of an array.

```
var i = 0;
while (i < parks.length) {
  alert("Element " + i + " is " + parks[i]);
  i++
}
```

The output is:

```
Element 0 is Yosemite
Element 1 is Yellowstone
Element 2 is Grand Canyon
```

A more-compact for loop is often preferred for iterating through arrays:

```
for (var i = 0; i < parks.length; i++) {
  alert("Element " + i + " is " + parks[i]);
}
```

Because the looping condition is i < parks.length rather than i < 3, the loop works for arrays of any length. The variables i, j, and k are often used as loop counters.

The following for loop sums all the elements of an array.

```javascript
var sum = 0;
for (var i = 0; i < primes.length; i++) {
  sum += primes[i];
}
alert("The sum is " + sum);
```

The output is:

```
The sum is 77
```

The following program uses a regular expression (page 66) and nested loops to print only the vowels of each element of an array of strings.

```javascript
var vowels = /[aeiou]/;    // Regular expression
for (var i = 0, string, vowelsOnly; i < parks.length; i++) {
  string = parks[i];
  vowelsOnly = "";    // Reset for each new string
  for (var j = 0, ch; j < string.length; j++) {
    ch = string.charAt(j);    // Get the next character
    if (vowels.test(ch)) {    // Is it a vowel?
      vowelsOnly += ch;        // Concatenate with other vowels
    }
  }
  alert("string = " + string + ", vowelsOnly = " + vowelsOnly);
}
```

The output is:

```
string = Yosemite, vowelsOnly = oeie
string = Yellowstone, vowelsOnly = eooe
string = Grand Canyon, vowelsOnly = aao
```

Working with Arrays

The real strength of arrays are their built-in array properties and methods. You've seen the length property. The following examples demonstrate commonly used array methods.

```javascript
var fruits = ["Pear", "Apple", "Mango"];
```

The push() method adds one or more elements to the end of an array.

```javascript
fruits.push("Peach");  // ["Pear", "Apple", "Mango", "Peach"]
```

The pop() method removes the last element from an array.

```javascript
fruits.pop();  // ["Pear", "Apple", "Mango"]
```

The shift() method removes the first element from an array.

```javascript
fruits.shift();  // ["Apple", "Mango"]
```

The `unshift()` method adds one or more elements to the beginning of an array.

```javascript
fruits.unshift("Lime");   // ["Lime", "Apple", "Mango"]
```

The `indexOf()` method returns the first index at which a specified element can be found in an array, or –1 if it's not found.

```javascript
var pos = fruits.indexOf("Mango");   // 2
```

The `join()` method joins all elements of an array into a string. (You can also use the `toString()` method to return a string representing the elements of an array.)

```javascript
var str = fruits.join(", ");   // Lime, Apple, Mango (string)
```

The `sort()` method sorts the elements of an array in place.

```javascript
fruits.sort();   // ["Apple", "Lime", "Mango"]
```

The `reverse()` method reverses the order of elements of an array in place, putting the last element first, the next-to-last element second, and so on. Array reversal often is done to reverse an array after it's been sorted with `sort()`.

```javascript
fruits.reverse();   // ["Mango", "Lime", "Apple"]
```

More array methods are available. You don't have to memorize all this information. Eventually, you'll memorize the methods that you use frequently, but no programmer tries to memorize every property and method of every object. Instead, find a reference guide. For JavaScript, I prefer the Mozilla Foundation's JavaScript reference at *developer.mozilla.org/en/docs/Web/JavaScript/Reference*. (Mozilla produces the Firefox web browser.)

Arrays and Collections in Other Languages

Every programming language supports arrays and other types of collections, and they can differ from JavaScript arrays in the following ways.

- **Single data types.** JavaScript permits mixed data types in the same array: numbers, strings, booleans, undefined values, and so on. But many (or most) other languages allow only a specific type of data in a given array—you must declare an array that contains only strings or only integers, for example.

- **Fixed-size arrays.** JavaScript lets you add and remove array elements, but some other languages require an array to be a fixed size, meaning you must know how many elements an array contains (and will always contain) when you declare it. If you declare an array that contains five elements, then you can change the values of those elements, but not the number of elements. Variable-size arrays are called **mutable**, and fixed-size arrays are **immutable**. Some languages let you choose whether an array is mutable or immutable. Immutable arrays are less flexible than mutable arrays, but they have some advantages. You'd probably use an immutable array to store the days of the week or the months of the year, for example, because you wouldn't want to add or remove elements mid-program. Immutable arrays are faster to access and update because the language can allocate a fixed area of memory for storing array elements, whereas mutable arrays incur additional processing overhead because they can grow or shrink.

- **Associative arrays.** Arrays use zero-based indexes: the first element is at index zero, the second is at index one, and so on. In an **associative array**, each element is accessed not by an index number but by a unique identifier that you assign, called a **key**. Each value and its associated key is called a **key-value pair**. Associative arrays are also called hashes, dictionaries, maps, or tables. The following associative array, named `states`, contains the names of U.S. states indexed by their two-letter postal abbreviations. The expression `states["AZ"]` returns `"Arizona"`.

"Alabama"	"Alaska"	"Arizona"	. . .	"Wyoming"

| "AL" | "AK" | "AZ" | . . . | "WY" |

CHAPTER 8

Programming Style & Pseudocode

Adopting a Programming Style

Coding conventions vary among programmers and organizations. A set of rules or guidelines used when writing source code is called a programming **style guide**.

When you start programming in a new language, it's a good practice to adopt an established or popular style guide. You can modify it over time to suit your own preferences. To find JavaScript style guides, search the web for *javascript style guide*. Most of the examples in this book follow the guidelines in Google's JavaScript style guide at *google.github.io/styleguide/javascriptguide.xml*, but you can adopt your own style as you gain experience. Software development and IT departments in many organizations either create a custom in-house style guide or adopt a publicly available one as their own.

Style guidelines strive to make code easier to read and maintain. They typically cover:

- Naming and declaring variables, functions, and objects
- Using whitespace, comments, and indentation
- Using parentheses ( ), braces { }, and brackets [ ]
- Line length and line breaks
- General programming practices and principles

Naming Conventions

Recall that names in JavaScript must be written as one word (no spaces) that contains only:

- Letters (a–z, A–Z)
- Digits (0, 1, 2,…, 9)
- Dollar signs ($)
- Underscores (_)

No other characters are allowed, and names can't begin with a digit. These rules permit names like _ABC_$$re45g, but you want your code to be clear and readable. When you're learning to program, placeholder names like a, b, x, y, str, and foo are common, but readable programs use meaningful names like employeeLastName, imageWidth, customerId, payDate, sum, temp, and createMessage. Short names should be meaningful within their context: i, j, and k are often used as loop counters, for example, and x, y, and z are easily understood in the context of a 3D surface.

In JavaScript, the dominant naming style for variables and functions is **camel case**, called so because the uppercase letters in variableNamesLikeThis resemble the humps of a camel. If a name has only one word, then use all lowercase letters: count, price, i, and so on. Every mainstream JavaScript style guide recommends the use of camel case variable and function names, and JavaScript itself uses camel case for built-in function, method, property, and parameter names. The dominant naming style in some other languages is lowercase_names_with_underscores. Names with uppercase letters or underscores are easier to read than nameswithoutthem. See also "Naming Functions" on page 54.

Brace Placement

JavaScript, like all C-style languages, is a free-form language without many rules about how to format statements. The three most popular styles for placing braces in block statements {...} are:

```
if (condition) {          if (condition)           if (condition)
  block                   {                          {
}                           block                    block
                          }                          }
```

The first style, with the opening brace on the same line as the keyword (if, while, for, and so on), is the dominant style in JavaScript, but plenty of programmers use the other styles. Whichever style you choose, use it consistently in your programs.

Odds & Ends

Here are some other important JavaScript style guidelines:

- Always declare variables with `var` (page 23).

- Define functions before you call them (page 58).

- Always end a statement with a semicolon. Relying on JavaScript to insert implicit statement terminators can cause subtle, hard-to-find problems.

- If a statement exceeds eighty characters in length, then split it over multiple lines.

Writing Pseudocode

Before creating a new program or function, consider stepping away from your computer and writing pseudocode on a piece of paper or a whiteboard. Pseudocode is an informal, high-level description of computer instructions written in natural (casual) language. Pseudocode isn't a programming language but it uses the structural conventions of one while omitting syntactic details like variable declarations, case sensitivity, parentheses, and curly braces. It's commonly used to sketch out the structure of a program before the actual coding begins.

Pseudocode doesn't have formal rules, but it should be readable by anyone who understands the problem, whether or not that person can program. The following pseudocode describes the procedure for acquiring a user-entered email address.

```
ask user for email address
if email address matches accepted pattern
  add address to email list
else
  show error message
```

Readable, uncluttered pseudocode defines only the general structure of code. One line of pseudocode isn't one line of real code. Don't subdivide:

```
ask user for email address
```

into:

```
declare email variable
ask user for email address
store user's email address in email variable
```

It's common to indent statements and use keywords like `if`, `else`, `while`, and `for` in pseudocode. Different people write pseudocode in different ways. The longer that someone's been programming in a language, the more their pseudocode tends to mimic the style of that language.

Some programmers use uppercase words to demarcate loops and conditional statements. A phrase like END IF or END LOOP can serve the same purpose as a closing brace in JavaScript or another C-style language.

```
IF balance < 0
  print "negative balance"
ELSE
  do nothing
END IF
```

The following pseudocode describes the procedure for calculating the sum of the squares of numbers in a list.

```
set sumsquares to zero

get list of numbers

loop through each number in the list
  square each number
  add each square to sumsquares
end loop

return sumsquares
```

Pseudocode isn't just for beginners. Experienced software developers use it to discover potential problems and knowledge gaps prior to writing code. Suppose that you write the following snippet of pseudocode for a racing game.

```
if car-image touches massive-object-image
  replace car-image with explosion-image
  play explosion sound
  if remaining-lives counter is zero
    print "game over"
    play game-over sound
  else
    subtract 1 from remaining-lives counter
    redraw car-image in most recent position
    play idling-engine sound
    ...
```

If you realize that you don't know how to play a sound in the language or system you're working with, then add that task to your to-do list ("research how to play sounds") and continue writing pseudocode.

CHAPTER 9

Input & Output

Input, Output & Persistence

The concepts of input and output have changed over the years. Decades ago, all programs were **batch** programs, meaning they accepted an input file containing data, processed it, and then returned the results in an output file or sent them directly to a printer. You didn't interact with a batch program while it was running. We still have batch programs, mostly in the form of command-line utilities and other specialized tools that run and finish quickly, but now most programs run with interactive graphical user interfaces. A web browser, for example, doesn't start, run, and then suddenly stop. It stays up and running while you interact with it continually and unpredictably for hours, days, or weeks.

Consequently, the concepts of input and output have expanded beyond reading and writing files. A mouse click is input, text typed in a webpage is input, changing onscreen text or images is output, and playing video or audio is output. For more examples of input and output, see "Getting Input" on page 16.

Despite all these types of input and output, most computer work still involves working with **persistent** information, meaning stored data that outlives the currently running program. Persistent information includes data stored in a database, settings and user preferences stored on your smartphone, and documents saved on your local hard drive, on a server, or in the cloud. After you close the program or turn off your device, this data persists in the state that you left it.

All the variables that we've worked with so far don't persist. They're stored in your computer's volatile memory in RAM while the program is running. When you stop the program or the program stops by itself, the variables and their values all disappear.

Different programming languages support persistence in different ways, and JavaScript barely supports it at all. JavaScript has no statements or functions that can save files to, say, your Documents folder. That's intentional for security reasons. JavaScript was designed to be embedded in webpages, and you don't want webpages that you happen to visit saving files directly to your hard drive. General-purpose languages and languages designed for developing desktop or mobile applications can open or save files on a drive. They often have a variety of statements to do so and we'll look at a few of these features later in this chapter, but first we'll look at JavaScript input and output.

The Document Object Model

I've been using JavaScript so far to illustrate the basics of programming: variables, assignments, conditions, loops, functions, arrays, and so on. But JavaScript isn't a general-purpose programming language like C or Java. Real-world JavaScript is used to work with webpages. Such specialization is common. Programming languages are designed to work best in a particular environment. If you're writing an iPhone application in Swift, then you'll find functions that let you handle what happens when the phone rings while your program is running. If you're writing a Windows desktop application in a .NET language (C# or Visual Basic), then you'll find functions for dealing with printers and USB ports and multiple displays.

JavaScript's world is the webpage that loaded it, and it provides functions for inspecting and manipulating the content of webpages. JavaScript uses the **Document Object Model**, or **DOM**, to do so. The DOM is closely linked to HTML (Hypertext Markup Language), the standard markup language used to create webpages. The term Document Object Model sounds a bit abstract but it's a simple idea. The best way to understand it is to take it one word at a time:

- **Document.** In the context of the DOM, the document is the current webpage; that is, the webpage that loaded the JavaScript. In programming, it's perfectly allowable to represent the same document in different ways. In this case, a web browser loads an HTML file and renders it as a webpage, and both the HTML code and the browser view are considered to be the same document.

- **Object.** An object is an element, or component, of the document. In the browser (webpage) view of a document, an object might be the headline, the second bullet point, the second letter of the third word,

Two Representations of the Same Document

The following HTML code is rendered by a browser as the webpage shown below. In the Document Object Model, both views are different representations of the same document.

```
<html>
  <head>
    <title>Learning JavaScript</title>
  </head>
  <body>
    <h1>JavaScript Basics</h1>
    <p>JavaScript is:</p>
    <ul>
      <li>An interpreted programming language</li>
      <li>A core technology for producing web content</li>
      <li>Supported by all modern web browsers</li>
    </ul>
  </body>
</html>
```

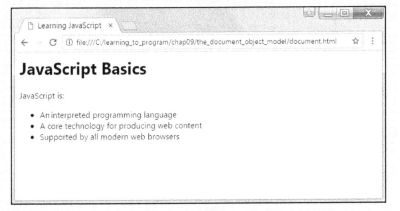

or even the entire page. In the HTML (code) view of a document, an object might be the headline element <h1>...</h1>, an unordered list element <ul>...</ul>, a particular list item element <li>...</li>, or the entire document element <html>...</html>. Note that objects can contain other objects. Via the DOM, JavaScript can access every object at every nesting level, from the entire document to the smallest element.

- **Model.** The model describes individual elements and their hierarchy, relationships, and interactions in a standard way, described next.

By using the DOM, you can write JavaScript that interacts with any webpage. For example, you can write JavaScript that:

- Gets the title text

- Gets the third paragraph

- Changes the background color of all paragraphs

- Gets all the items in a list

- Moves the image named "logo" fifty pixels to the left

- Makes the second link in a menu invisible

- Changes a link so that it runs a JavaScript function when clicked

- Creates a list and inserts it between the second and third paragraphs

The DOM provides a standard way to reach into a webpage from JavaScript code, and vice versa. Suppose that I have a folder that contains the files script.js (JavaScript code) and simple.html (an HTML document). The file script.js is empty (for now) and the file simple.html contains the following HTML code.

```html
<html>
  <head>
    <title>Simple Webpage</title>
  </head>
  <body>
    <h1 id="mainHeading">My Original Headline</h1>
    <p>This is a simple webpage.</p>
    <script src="script.js"></script>
  </body>
</html>
```

The `id` attribute specifies a unique identifier for an HTML element (the value must be unique within the HTML document). Here, I've set the `id` attribute to the value `"mainHeading"` to identify the `<h1>` element uniquely in the page. The `<script>` element points to the (empty) file script.js. Opening simple.html in a browser shows the following webpage.

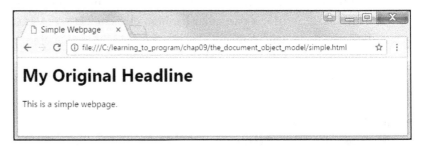

Next, I open script.js in a text editor, type the following JavaScript statements, and then save and close the file.

```
var headline = document.getElementById("mainHeading");
headline.innerHTML = "A New Headline";
```

When an HTML document is loaded into a web browser, it becomes a **document object**. The document object, named document, "owns" all the other page elements and provides properties and methods to access them from within JavaScript. The getElementById(*elementId*) method returns the element that has the specified id attribute value. (getElementById() is one of the most frequently used methods in all of JavaScript.) Here, the first JavaScript statement gets the element with the identifier mainHeading (that is, <h1>) via the DOM and stores its reference in the variable headline. The second JavaScript statement uses the innerHTML property to set the HTML content of the headline element.

Reloading simple.html in the browser runs script.js (specified by the <script> element in simple.html) and shows the following webpage.

The headline changes in the browser view but not in the actual HTML code. The content of <h1> in simple.html is still My Original Headline. You can use other JavaScript properties and methods to change any webpage element via the DOM.

All programming languages have a specialized world in which they work best. Mastery of the DOM is the single most important skill in JavaScript.

Event-Driven Programming

All our JavaScript code so far executes as soon as the webpage loads the script file. The code loads, runs, and then finishes. We used the prompt() function once or twice to get user input, but otherwise we've ignored the user. Now we want to write code that responds to the user. User actions are called events, and writing code that responds to them is called **event-driven programming**. JavaScript, like many modern languages, can respond to events.

An event can be something the browser does, or something a user does. Events include:

- Loading a page

- Typing on the keyboard (each key press and release is a separate event)

- Clicking a mouse button

- Moving the mouse pointer (mouse movements trigger multiple events)

- Resizing a window

- Scrolling a window

- Dragging an object

- Tabbing into or out of an input field

- Cutting, copying, or pasting content

- Leaving a page

Many more events exist, and as a programmer you must decide which ones you care about. The code examples so far run only when the page loads, but event-driven programming lets you write functions that run only when, say, the user clicks an image or tabs to a specific field.

Your code doesn't need to ask continuously whether the user is clicking a button or typing in a text box. The operating system takes care of that. You need only to write **event handlers**, or **event listeners**, that run when specific events happen. Event handlers can be used to handle and verify user input, user actions, and browser actions. In JavaScript, events are designated by lowercase keywords that begin with the word "on". Common events include:

- onblur—An HTML element loses focus (a user exits an input field)

- onchange—An HTML element changes

- onclick—A user clicks an HTML element

- onfocus—An HTML element gets focus (a user enters an input field)

- ondrag—A user drags an HTML element

- onmouseover—A user moves the mouse pointer over an HTML element

- onmouseout—A user moves the mouse pointer away from an HTML element

- onkeydown—A user pushes a keyboard key

- onload—The browser finishes loading the page

- onunload—A user navigates away from the page

You can write functions and hook them up to specific events. One event can call multiple functions, or multiple events can call the same function.

Events can occur on different page elements. An `onclick` event can be a click on a specific button, image, or paragraph, for example. Consequently, event syntax specifies an element name and an event name:

element.event

For example, the load event of the window element is:

```
window.onload
```

The window here represents the browser window. You can react to this event when the page loads.

If a page has a form with user-editable text fields, then the handler:

```
lastNameField.onblur
```

is triggered, or fired, when the user exits the "Last Name" field by clicking out of the field or pressing the Tab key.

One of the most common handlers is:

element.onclick

where *element* is a variable that refers to a specific page element that you've retrieved by using the DOM. *element* can be any clickable element: a heading, an image, a paragraph, and so on. In the preceding section, for example, we used the variable `headline` to refer to a page's main heading (`<h1>` element):

```
var headline = document.getElementById("mainHeading");
```

The typical syntax of an event handler is:

```
element.event = function() {
  // event handler code
  // ...
  // ...
};
```

The event handler for the `onclick` event of `headline`, for example, is:

```
headline.onclick = function() {
  // event handler code
  // ...
  // ...
};
```

The event handler uses an **anonymous function**, meaning a function that has no (and needs no) name. Anonymous functions are used frequently in JavaScript. A semicolon follows the closing brace because this event handler is a *statement*, not a function. Specifically, it's an assignment statement (note the assignment operator =), so it needs a terminating semicolon.

You have several ways to handle an event in JavaScript. The following example illustrates the general principle. Start with the same setup as in the preceding section: a folder that contains the files script.js (JavaScript code) and simple.html (an HTML document). The file simple.html contains the same HTML code as last time:

```
<html>
  <head>
    <title>Simple Webpage</title>
  </head>
  <body>
    <h1 id="mainHeading">My Original Headline</h1>
    <p>This is a simple webpage.</p>
    <script src="script.js"></script>
  </body>
</html>
```

And opening simple.html in a browser shows the same webpage:

But in this example, the innerHTML assignment in script.js is placed in an event handler:

```
var headline = document.getElementById("mainHeading");

headline.onclick = function() {
  headline.innerHTML = "You Clicked The Headline";
};
```

In the preceding section, the headline changed immediately when the page was loaded. In this example, the event handler changes the headline only when the headline itself (the <h1> element) is clicked. All other events are ignored. You can click elsewhere on the page, resize the window, move the mouse around—nothing happens to the headline until you click it:

File I/O

We saw earlier that for security reasons standard JavaScript can't access files on your hard drive or on a private server. In practice, however, it's often necessary to access files from within a program to read, write, and manipulate stored data. File input and output is a crucial programming skill, so let's look at how it's done in the programming language Python (*python.org*). The operating system manages your files, and Python's file I/O tools let you access them from inside programs. The following Python code opens a file and prints its contents line by line.

```
filename = "infile.txt"
f = open(filename, "r")
for line in f:
  print line
f.close()
```

Python file operations are done by using file objects rather than file names. Before you can read from or write to a file, you must open it as a file object. The open(*filename, mode*) function opens a file and returns a file object. *filename* is a file name (string) that can include a relative or absolute path (folder location); if no path is given, Python looks in the current folder. *mode* is a string that indicates how the file is to be opened—for reading, writing, or both. Here, I'm opening the file in read-only ("r") mode because I don't want to change the file's contents.

Despite the apparent simplicity of accessing a file, things can and often do go wrong. When you're dealing with file I/O, you'll find yourself writing a lot of conditional code just to prevent disaster. Some common reasons that file operations fail are:

- Trying to open a nonexistent file ("file not found")

- Trying to open a huge file that won't fit in a variable or in memory

- Trying to open a file that another program already has open or locked

- Trying to write to a file opened for reading

- Trying to open a read-only file for writing

- Lacking permission to access a file

In this simple example, I'm not worrying about errors. I'm just reading a small text file that I know exists.

The for loop reads through the file line by line until the end of the file. In each loop iteration, the string variable line is set implicitly to the text of the current line of the file. The for loop's body is a single print statement, which prints the current line.

Python file modes

Mode	Description
"r"	Only read from the file. *filename* must already exist.
"w"	Only write to the file. If *filename* doesn't already exist, it's created; otherwise, *filename*'s existing contents are overwritten.
"a"	Only append to the file. If *filename* doesn't already exist, it's created; new data is appended to the end of *filename*.
"r+"	Read from and write to the file. *filename* must already exist.
"w+"	Read from and write to the file. If *filename* doesn't already exist, it's created; otherwise, *filename*'s existing contents are deleted before writing.
"a+"	Read from and write to the file. If *filename* doesn't already exist, it's created; new data is appended to the end of *filename*.

Python is the rare language that's sensitive to whitespace (spaces and tabs) at the beginning of lines. Python uses indentation to group statements into code blocks. The `print` statement is indented below the `for` statement and thus forms the `for` loop's body. The next unindented statement, `f.close()`, marks the end of the block. Most languages use curly braces or begin/end keywords to demarcate code blocks. Also note that the end of the line marks the end of a statement. Python statements don't need a trailing semicolon or other explicit statement terminator (unless multiple statements are placed on the same line).

The `f.close()` statement closes the file. When you're finished reading from or writing to files, you should close them to free memory. Closing files isn't strictly required because Python closes them automatically when the program finishes, but leaving files open unnecessarily occupies resources that Python could otherwise reclaim.

The following Python code opens a file and writes a string to it.

```
message = "Hello, world!\n"
filename = "outfile.txt"
f = open(filename, "a")
f.write(message)
f.close()
```

I'm opening the file outfile.txt in append (`"a"`) mode because I want to add the string `message` to the end of the file. If I opened the file in write (`"w"`) mode, then Python would erase the existing contents of outfile.txt before writing to it.

The `write()` method writes the specified string to an open file. This method doesn't insert a new line or carriage return at the end of the string, so I've added a new line escape character (`\n`) to `message`. Escape characters in Python and JavaScript work in the same way (page 34).

Finally, I close the file when I'm finished writing to it.

Other languages support the same file I/O concepts and operations in slightly different ways, and they have built-in functions for reading and writing files. Python is one of the simplest languages in this regard. The equivalent code in C++, Java, or C# would require more explanation. Languages can read and write text files and binary data files like audio or video.

Small files aside, programmers rarely read an entire file all at once. Instead, they read and process them in pieces, chunk by chunk. Text files are typically read one line at a time and binary files are often read a fixed number of bytes at a time. Each piece is processed in a `while` or `for` loop until the file ends or some other condition is satisfied. If you're searching for the string "Brooks" in a file that contains an alphabetical list of names, then you're going to exit the loop when that value is found rather than continuing to the end of the file.

CHAPTER 10

Errors & Debugging

Types of Errors

Programming languages differ from natural (spoken) languages in that programming languages are designed for a specific purpose, have a small vocabulary, and are inflexible and unambiguous. So if you don't get the results you expect, it's because your program contains an error, or **bug**, and not because the computer misinterpreted your instructions. Debugging one's programs is a cardinal programming task.

JavaScript, like any formal language, is defined by rules of **syntax**, which determine the words and symbols you can use and how they can be combined, and **semantics**, which determine the actual meaning of a syntactically correct statement. Note that you can write a legal statement that expresses the wrong meaning (good syntax, bad semantics).

If you've never written a program before, then you'll find the transition from natural to formal language to be frustrating. Many beginners find it challenging to write even a single line of code that works correctly. Programming languages are so specific that it's easy to use a colon instead of a semicolon, type letters in the wrong case, forget to end a string with a closing quote, use the wrong operator, or misspell a word. The mistakes multiply as you progress beyond Hello World-level programs to nontrivial code.

Here's a tip from the pros: don't expect your code to work correctly the first time. Ever. Experienced programmers never expect it, and neither should you. Working programs aren't simply typed into existence. They're built slowly, line by line, function by function. Every programmer spends far more time testing and debugging code than actually writing it. They write a few statements, test them, fix them, write a few more, test them, fix them, return to earlier code that broke because of the latest fix, and so on.

Debugging spans the entire development process, from getting a program to run for the first time to a year later when it's suddenly behaving oddly after you thought it was working fine.

Coding errors fall into two main categories: syntax errors and logic errors.

Syntax Errors

The most obvious type of bug is a **syntax error**, which violates one of the grammatical rules that defines how tokens can be used and combined to form a valid expression or statement. Tokens (page 17) include names, keywords, literals, operators, delimiters, and escape characters. Here are a few common syntax errors:

```
Alert("Hello, world!");   // Wrong case letter used in keyword

alert("Hello, world!);    // String has no closing quote

alert("Hello, world!');   // String has mixed quotes " and '

alert("Hello, world!"):   // Statement ends with ":", not ";"

alert("Hello, world!");   // Keyword spelled with "1", not "l"

alert("Hello, world!";    // Function has no closing ")"
```

Syntax errors are easy to spot and fix when you're looking at a few lines of code, but most of the time you'll be reading hundreds or thousands of lines that look like this:

```
// show or hide greeting div element
function toggleGreeting() {
  document.getElementById("greetme").onclick = function() {
    if (document.getElementById("greetme").checked) {
      // set property to show div...
      document.getElementById("greeting").style.display =
        "block";
    } else {
      // ...or hide it
      document.getElementById("greeting").style.display =
        "none";
    }
  };
  // show greeting on initial page load
  document.getElementById("greeting").style.display = "block";
}

window.onload = function() {
  toggleGreeting();
};
```

Even experienced programmers sometimes pore through code character by character. It's common to count opening and closing braces, brackets, and parentheses to make sure that they're paired correctly.

One of the benefits that a programmer's text editor (page 6) provides is syntax highlighting, which color-codes different parts of the language (strings, keywords, comments, on so on). Suppose that your editor displays strings in green. If you omit or delete the closing quote of a string, then the editor will instantly change the color of the following lines to green because it considers them to be part of one long string (until it encounters the next quote in your code, which it will interpret as the closing quote). A similar color change will happen if you accidentally open a multiline comment (/*) instead of a single-line comment (//). As you type, it's common to see a screenful of code suddenly change color, alerting you to these types of syntax errors.

One of the benefits of using a compiled language rather than an interpreted language (page 8) is that the compiler detects syntax errors before you even try to run the program. With an interpreted language such as JavaScript, you often have to try to run the program to find out what's wrong. As you become familiar with a language, you'll make fewer syntax errors.

Logic Errors

A program with a logic error is a valid (syntactically correct) program that runs but doesn't behave as intended. The only clue to the existence of logic errors is that the program produces incorrect or undesired results. Compilers and interpreters may sometimes warn you about valid but suspicious code (like the use of an assignment as a condition) but in general they don't—and can't—detect flaws in logic. Let's look at some common logic errors.

An **off-by-one error** causes a loop to iterate one time too many or too few. The following for loop sums the elements of an array incorrectly because the looping condition i <= array.length iterates one time too many (passed the end of the array). The correct condition is i < array.length.

```
for (var i = 0, sum = 0; i <= array.length; i++) {
  sum += array[i];
}
```

The following function calculates the average of two numbers incorrectly because of operator precedence (page 29). Division is evaluated before addition; the correct expression is (x + y) / 2.

```
function average(x, y) {
  return x + y / 2;
}
```

We've seen other types of logic errors and the programming practices that can cause them, including:

- Using undefined variables or creating variables without var (page 23)

- Misusing increment (++) or decrement (––) operators in postfix and prefix assignments (page 27)

- Comparing for equality (==, !=) when strict equality (===, !==) is called for (page 38)

- Combining comparison and logical operators incorrectly (page 39)

- Using assignments as conditions (page 42)

- Forgetting a break in a switch statement (page 44)

- Creating an infinite loop (page 47)

- Writing unreachable code (page 56)

- Using global variables excessively or unintentionally (page 57)

- Opening a file in the wrong mode (page 87)

- Using a faulty algorithm (page 107)

- Failing to handle nonsensical input data

- Making arithmetic errors

Arithmetic errors are especially common. JavaScript uses NaN (page 62) and Infinity (page 63) to recover gracefully from undefined mathematical operations like dividing by zero and calculating the log or square root of a negative real number. But in many other programming languages these errors will crash the program.

The preceding examples are just a few of the many ways that things can go wrong. Logic errors can be extremely difficult to find, and they'll be your biggest problem as a programmer. The first step in any debugging situation is to reproduce the problem. Does the same error occur in the same way every time? If so, you're in luck because that makes the bug easier to squash. Next, figure out where in your code the problem actually occurs, which is often harder than it sounds. For that, you can trace through your code (page 93) or use a debugger (page 97).

Tracing Through Code

Tracing through code is a basic debugging technique that determines how code executes. Tracing takes many forms, including reading a hardcopy printout of the code line by line, pretending you're the computer. We're going to look at the common practice of adding "print" statements to suspect code. In JavaScript, we've been using the `alert()` function to print data and messages. Other languages have similar statements that print or log messages: C has `printf()`, Java has `println()`, Python has `print`, Ruby has `puts`, and so on.

Tip: Most JavaScript programmers regard pop-up dialog boxes as annoying, and so use `console.log()` rather than `alert()`. The `console.log()` method prints information in the browser's console (page 96).

We'll start with the same setup as in the preceding chapter: a folder that contains the files script.js (JavaScript code) and simple.html (an HTML document). The file simple.html contains the following HTML code.

```html
<html>
  <head>
    <title>Simple Webpage</title>
  </head>
  <body>
    <h1 id="mainHeading">My Original Headline</h1>
    <p>This is a simple webpage.</p>
    <script src="script.js"></script>
  </body>
</html>
```

Opening simple.html in a browser shows the following webpage. The HTML code in simple.html points to script.js via the `<script>` element.

The file script.js contains the following JavaScript code.

```javascript
function myFunctionOne() {
  myFunctionTwo();
}

function myFunctionTwo() {
  myFunctionThree();
}

function myFunctionThree() {
  myFunctionfour();
}

function myFunctionFour() {
  headline.innerHTML = "You Clicked The Headline";
}

var headline = document.getElementById("mainHeading");
headline.onclick = function() {
  myFunctionOne();
};
```

The functions myFunctionOne(), myFunctionTwo(), myFunctionThree(), and myFunctionFour() call each other in sequence, establishing a flow that we can trace. The final function changes the headline. The event handler starts the chain of function calls by calling myFunctionOne() when the headline (the <h1> element) is clicked. For details about event handlers, see "Event-Driven Programming" on page 83.

This code has a bug. Let's say that we don't see it. We open simple.html in a browser and it looks fine, but no matter how many times we click the headline, nothing happens. We switch back to the JavaScript code. Maybe we're grabbing the wrong headline element. Or maybe the event handler isn't even calling myFunctionOne(). Or maybe myFunctionOne() isn't calling myFunctionTwo(). And so on. We have no idea what's wrong. Perhaps the HTML code isn't even pointing to the right JavaScript file.

The low-tech way to find this bug is to trace through the code by inserting alert() functions at "interesting" locations, like just before function calls. If a particular alert message doesn't appear when you expect it or displays unexpected values, then that's where to look for the bug. In practice, you normally have an idea of where a bug occurs, so you'd insert only one or two alert() functions in that vicinity. In this example, we'll insert alert() functions throughout the code to illustrate the general principle.

```javascript
function myFunctionOne() {
  alert("About to call myFunctionTwo");
  myFunctionTwo();
}
```

```
function myFunctionTwo() {
  alert("About to call myFunctionThree");
  myFunctionThree();
}

function myFunctionThree() {
  alert("About to call myFunctionFour");
  myFunctionfour();
}

function myFunctionFour() {
  alert("About to change the headline");
  headline.innerHTML = "You Clicked The Headline";
}

var headline = document.getElementById("mainHeading");
headline.onclick = function() {
  alert("About to call myFunctionOne");
  myFunctionOne();
  alert("Finished calling myFunctionOne");
};
```

In the browser, reload simple.html (press F5) and then click the headline. The alert boxes start to appear in the expected order:

"About to call myFunctionOne"

"About to call myFunctionTwo"

"About to call myFunctionThree"

"About to call myFunctionFour"

And then the alerts stop. Aha! Something bad happened after this alert and before the next alert ("About to change the headline"). Inspecting the code reveals a typo inside myFunctionThree(): we're calling a nonexistent function named *myFunctionfour*. The correct name of the called function is *myFunctionFour*, with an uppercase *F* in *Four*. Fix the lowercase *f*, save the file, reload the webpage, and then click the headline. It changes. Problem solved. You can delete the alert() statements or comment them out if you think you'll need them again later.

Following the flow of a program by printing messages, also called **logging to the console**, is a very common debugging technique. It can be tedious and it's not something you'd do with ten thousand lines of code, but it's easy, works with all languages, and doesn't require special debugging tools. You'll often discover bugs just by inserting trace messages.

Opening the Console in Various Browsers

In Google Chrome, choose ⋮ > More Tools > Developer Tools > Console. Keyboard shortcut: Ctrl+Shift+J (Windows) or Command+Option+J (Mac).

In Mozilla Firefox, choose Tools > Web Developer > Web Console. Keyboard shortcut: Ctrl+Shift+K (Windows) or Command+Option+K (Mac).

In Microsoft Internet Explorer, choose Tools > F12 Developer Tools > Console. Keyboard shortcut: F12.

In Microsoft Edge, choose ••• > F12 Developer Tools > Console. Keyboard shortcut: F12.

In Apple Safari, choose Safari > Preferences > Advanced pane > select "Show Develop menu in menu bar". Close Preferences and then choose Develop > Show Error Console. Keyboard shortcut: Command+Option+C.

Viewing Error Messages

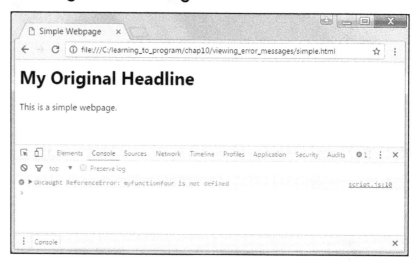

Most programming languages issue helpful warnings and error messages when you interpret, compile, or run a buggy program. JavaScript is one of the few languages that remains mute in this respect because of the way that it's used. If you have bugs in your JavaScript code, then you don't want error messages to scroll down the browser window of everyone who views your webpage.

Every modern browser has built-in developer tools. The **console**, which is hidden by default, lets you view error messages and other diagnostics. The console works similarly in every web browser. The following example uses the Google Chrome browser.

Let's revisit the bug from the preceding section. We have a folder that contains the files script.js (JavaScript code) and simple.html (an HTML document). simple.html contains the same HTML code and script.js contains the same error: `myFunctionThree()` calls the nonexistent function named *myFunctionfour* (the lowercase *f* should be uppercase—the correct function name is *myFunctionFour*). To view the message for this error in the console, do the following:

1. Open simple.html in Chrome.

2. Click the headline "My Original Headline".

   Note that no error message appears on the webpage itself.

3. To open Chrome's developer tools (DevTools), choose ⋮ > More Tools > Developer Tools. Keyboard shortcut: Ctrl+Shift+I (Windows) or Command+Option+I (Mac).

   The DevTools window opens in the browser, or possibly in its own window.

4. Click the Console tab.

An error message appears in the console: "Uncaught ReferenceError: myFunctionfour is not defined". This message repeats every time that you click the headline. To the right of the message is a link, "script.js:10", to the file and line number where the error occurred. To view the suspect code, click the link.

If your code has several errors, they'll all appear in the console. In general, you should fix multiple errors from the top down because early errors tend to generate later ones.

Using a Debugger

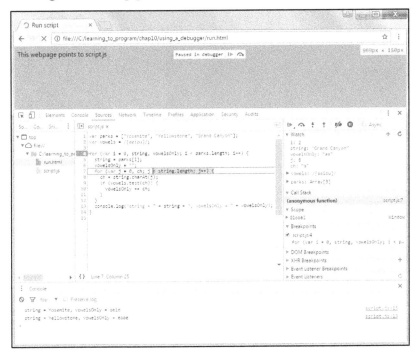

The console is only one of a browser's many built-in tools that help you debug and optimize code. Other tools provide web developers with deep access into the internals of the browser and their web applications. As the complexity of your JavaScript code increases, you'll need a debugger to help you find and fix problems. Using a debugger is more complex than tracing through code, but it makes debugging much less painful by helping you discover the causes of issues quickly and fix them efficiently. Though they provide similar features, debuggers operate differently across browsers, so you should read the developer documentation for your browser. To open Chrome's debugger, for example, choose ⋮ > More Tools > Developer Tools and then click the Sources tab. You can read Chrome's developer documentation at *developers.google.com/web/tools/chrome-devtools*.

Breakpoints

Why doesn't this line of code seem to have any effect? Why is this variable value 10 instead of 20? Why is this flag false when it should be true? Every developer faces questions like these. A debugger lets you execute code one line or one function at a time so that you can observe changes to understand exactly what's happening.

Using breakpoints is one of the most important debugging techniques in a developer's toolbox. A breakpoint tells the debugger to temporarily suspend execution of a program at a certain point. When the program hits a breakpoint and pauses, you can look for bugs by investigating the values of variables and the sequence of function calls at that moment in time.

In most browsers, you can set a breakpoint by clicking the left margin on a specific line of code in the debugger window. (Another type of breakpoint is triggered only when a specified condition is true.) When execution pauses, you can optionally step over, into, and out of functions calls. You can also create a watch list in the debugger's sidebar to easily see the current values of multiple variables throughout your program, eliminating the need to repeatedly log values to the console.

CHAPTER 11

Objects

Classes and Objects

Most programming languages created in the last few decades are object-oriented languages. Older languages, including C, Fortran, COBOL, and Pascal, are procedural languages, owing to their reliance on functions (procedures). Object-oriented languages support the use of self-contained objects. We've already seen a few of JavaScript's built-in objects, including the `Math` object (page 30) and `RegExp` objects (page 66). JavaScript, like all object-oriented programming languages, provides tools that you can use to create new types of objects. The notions of classes and objects are the bases for these tools.

A **class** is a template or blueprint for an **object**. Conceptually, classes are comparable to categories that you use to organize real-world information, such as *employee*, *vegetable*, or *chair*. In programs, you use a class to define a generalized category that describes a group of more-specific items (objects) that can exist within it. These objects have associated attributes and behaviors that characterize the object as a member of a class.

Object-oriented programming (OOP) is the use of programming techniques based on the concepts of classes and objects: you organize your program as a collection of discrete, self-contained objects that hold data and define behaviors that use that data or interact with other objects.

Object-oriented programming is a large topic, and this chapter provides only a brief introduction. Programming with objects takes practice, and it's important that you design a flexible and extensible class hierarchy in the early stages of your project. Programmers typically spend considerable time designing object-oriented programs before they write a line of code.

An object represents an instance of a distinguishable real-world entity, event, or concept. In your program, an object might be a specific student, employee, patient, player, image, movie, gene, car, bank account, weather condition, invoice, project, date, or appointment.

The terms *class* and *object* go hand in hand in object-oriented languages, and they represent the way that you actually think and talk about a problem. Keep in mind that a class defines an object's characteristics—it's not an object itself. An individual object is an **instance** of a certain class. An object myAssistant that belongs to a class Employee, for example, is an instance of the class Employee.

Object-oriented programming requires a shift in thinking that encompasses objects as well as processes. If you're writing a website for restaurant reviews, for example, then you might create classes that represent:

- A restaurant, a menu item, a review, a reviewer, a rating, or a user

- A visual or interactive element such as a text box, button, or window

- A price range, review counter, food type, or other well-defined concept

Object-oriented languages come with libraries of predefined classes, and let you define your own classes. A class characterizes objects by their attributes and behaviors. A class that describes a person, for example, would have attributes like name, height, weight, gender, and age, and behaviors like walk, run, jump, eat, speak, and sleep.

In JavaScript and many other object-oriented languages, attributes are called properties and behaviors are called methods. A **property** is a data value stored in a variable that belongs to only the current object (instance of a class). A **method** is a special kind of function that's defined in a class definition. An object uses its methods to perform actions that operate on its own data, such as printing itself. Contrast methods with ordinary functions (Chapter 5), which can handle different types of values and objects.

Object-Oriented Programming

The best way to become familiar with object-oriented programming is to use the built-in classes in your language to create objects. You can later define your own classes and create objects with them. You've actually already done this in JavaScript. When you defined an array (page 70), you created an array object:

```
var myArray = [1, 2, 3, 4, 5];
```

When you defined a regular expression (page 66), you created a regular expression object:

```
var myRE = /hello/;
```

Arrays and regular expressions are built-in classes in JavaScript. You can inspect and manipulate an array object by using properties like `length` and methods like `sort()` and `push()`. Regular expression objects have properties like `ignoreCase` and methods like `test()` and `replace()`.

Tip: Objects of the same class are independent of each other. You can have many array objects, for example, and work with each of them separately.

The built-in `Date` class is used to work with dates and times. The following statement creates, or **instantiates**, a new `Date` object. The variable `today` contains today's date as a `Date` object (not as a string).

```
var today = new Date();
```

You can also create a `Date` object for a specific date:

```
var newYear = new Date(2018, 0, 1);
```

Or for a specific date (year, month, day) and time (hours, minutes, seconds):

```
var myBirthdate = new Date(1982, 5, 22, 6, 35, 0);
```

Like all objects, `Date` objects have properties and methods that are accessed via the . (dot) operator. The "get" methods return an object's properties.

```
myBirthdate.getFullYear();    // 1982
myBirthdate.getMonth();       // 5 (0 == Jan, 1 == Feb, ...)
myBirthdate.getDate();        // 22 (1-31)
myBirthdate.getDay();         // 2 (0 == Sun, 1 == Mon, ...)
myBirthdate.getHours();       // 6 (0-23)
myBirthdate.getMinutes();     // 35 (0-59)
myBirthdate.getSeconds();     // 0 (0-59)
```

The "set" methods change an object's properties.

```
var myDate = new Date();
myDate.setFullYear(2018);     // 1000-9999
myDate.setMonth(11);          // 0 == Jan, 1 == Feb, ...
myDate.setDate(31);           // 1-31
myDate.toDateString();        // "Mon Dec 31 2018"
```

One of JavaScript's most frequently used built-in objects is the `Math` object, which has properties and methods for mathematical constants and functions. For details, see "The Math Object" on page 30.

You can consult a reference guide to read about JavaScript's other built-in classes. I prefer the Mozilla Foundation's JavaScript reference at *developer.mozilla.org/en/docs/Web/JavaScript/Reference*. JavaScript doesn't actually have that many built-in classes. Other languages, such as Java and C#, might have hundreds or even thousands of predefined classes, grouped into various categories.

Primitives

Number and boolean literals aren't objects; they're what are called primitives. Variables that store primitive data types are simple storage containers with no properties or methods.

```
// Number primitive
var myNumber = 123;
```

```
// Boolean primitive
var myBoolean = false;
```

Strings are objects in most object-oriented programming languages. In JavaScript, strings (Chapter 6) are technically primitives, but they behave like objects. JavaScript automatically converts string primitives to `String` objects, so it's possible to use `String` properties and methods with string primitives.

```
// String object
var myStr1 =
  new String("xyz");
myStr1.length    // 3
myStr1.charAt(1) // y
```

```
// String primitive
var myStr2 = "xyz";
myStr2.length    // OK: 3
myStr2.charAt(1) // OK: y
```

String primitives and `String` objects give different results in certain infrequent circumstances. In general, you needn't worry about the distinction, but be aware that your code may break if it encounters a `String` object when it expects a string primitive.

Note that JavaScript's built-in class names start with an uppercase letter (Date, RegExp, Math). This naming style helps you quickly distinguish class names from variable and function names, which by convention start with lowercase letters (page 76). This style is used in most object-oriented languages. When you create your own classes, you should adopt this style too.

JavaScript provides shortcuts for creating certain types of objects. The statements in the following pairs are equivalent, for example.

```
var myRE = /hello/;
var myRE = new RegExp("hello");

var myArray = [1, 2, 3, 4, 5];
var myArray = new Array(1, 2, 3, 4, 5);
```

The keyword new is used in many object-oriented languages to create a new instance of an object based on a class.

Object-Oriented Languages

Popular Object-Oriented Programming Languages

C++
C#
Java
JavaScript
Objective-C
Perl (since Perl 5)
PHP (since PHP 5)
Python
R
Ruby
Swift
Visual Basic .NET

Object-oriented programming is more of a concept than a strict set of criteria, so it's unclear which features are required to qualify as a true object-oriented language. Must everything in the language be an object? Or does the language merely need to support the creation of classes and objects? Such discussions are peppered with technical terms like polymorphism, composition, encapsulation, inheritance, and abstraction (which I won't go into). Support for objects varies across programming languages:

- C isn't an object-oriented language because its creation predates the concept of object-oriented programming

- C++ and Objective-C can be thought of as object-oriented versions of C

- C#, Java, and Swift are object-oriented languages that have many features of C

- Visual Basic .NET is the object-oriented version of its procedural predecessor, Visual Basic

- Perl and PHP were not originally object-oriented languages, but now support some object-oriented features

- Python, R, and JavaScript are object-oriented but can also be used as procedural languages

- Ruby is a thoroughly object-oriented language

Unless you're going to program in only C, you must become familiar with object-oriented programming. When you first learn an object-oriented language, determine what built-in classes it provides. A large library of classes means less work for you—somebody else already did the work.

In the JavaScript examples above, classes represent simple objects like arrays and dates. But languages such as Java, C#, and Swift have large and varied libraries of built-in classes for user-interface controls, media players, charts, images, cryptography, and much more.

The stricter the language is regarding object-orientation, the more your code will involve classes and objects. In Java, C#, Visual Basic .NET, Objective-C, and Swift, for example, you can't avoid object-orientation.

Advanced Topics

You can use a built-in system monitoring tool to determine whether a third-party application has a memory leak. Start a fresh session by closing the suspect app and then reopening it in a "neutral" state, with no open documents or tabs. Open Task Manager (Windows) or Activity Monitor (Mac) and then record the memory allocated to the app. Use the app normally for a day or so and then close all the documents or tabs (don't close the app itself). Open the system monitoring tool again and check the app's memory allocation. If it's substantially higher then it was when you started the session, then it leaks.

Memory Management

Memory management is the act of dynamically allocating blocks of memory (RAM) to programs at their request, and freeing those blocks for reuse when no longer needed. We haven't talked about memory management so far because it's unnecessary in JavaScript. We create variables and objects, use them, and then forget about them. In several languages, however, you must manage objects for their entire lifetime, from creation to destruction. The pseudocode for this process is:

```
allocate memory
create object
use object
free memory
```

The `allocate memory` instruction reserves a block of memory of specified size and returns a pointer (reference) to the beginning of that block. The `create object` instruction creates the object and stores it in the allocated block of memory, accessed via the pointer. When the program is finished using the object, the `free memory` instruction releases the object's block of memory back to the system.

Though it looks simple at first glance, memory management is quite difficult when you're passing around thousands of objects and calling hundreds of functions in a long-lived program. A common programming error is omitting the `free memory` instruction after an object is no longer needed, causing a **memory leak**. One or two memory leaks usually aren't a problem in a short-lived utility program, but a leaky long-lived program will become slower and slower as it runs, claiming more and more memory without releasing it. At some point the program may crash for lack of resources, or cause other programs to run slowly as it hogs resources.

Another common deallocation error involves dangling pointers. When you free memory for an object, that object is destroyed and its pointer then points to the location of the deallocated memory. The contents of freed memory are unpredictable because the system can reallocate that memory at any time to another process. A pointer that doesn't point to a valid object is a **dangling pointer**. If you think that a destroyed object still exists and use its pointer, then your program's behavior is unpredictable (it may crash or it may give wrong results).

Many languages have automated features that help you avoid memory leaks and other deallocation errors.

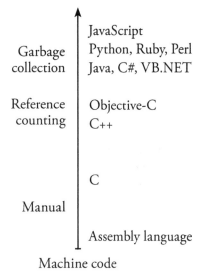

- Low-level languages (page 4) like assembly language and C provide no automated memory-management features. You must allocate and free memory manually. In C, for example, the relevant functions are `malloc()`, `realloc()`, `calloc()`, and `free()`.

- C++ and Objective-C use **reference counting**. This method tracks the number of references to each object. If an object's reference count reaches zero, then the system destroys that object and reclaims its memory. When an object is destroyed, any objects referenced by that object also have their reference counts decremented.

- Java, C#, and VB.NET use **garbage collection**. The system tracks how much memory the program is using. At certain times during the program's lifetime, the system scans the existing objects to determine which ones are still being used. Any object that's not being referenced is considered to be "garbage". It's destroyed and its memory is reclaimed. The system decides if and when garbage is collected. You can't force the garbage collector to run, but you can "suggest" that it do so.

- Scripting languages use either reference counting or garbage collection. Perl and Python use reference counting. Ruby and JavaScript use garbage collection. Scripting languages typically offer little or no manual control over when memory is reclaimed.

Reference counting and garbage collection free you from dealing with memory deallocation manually, resulting in fewer memory leaks and dangling-pointer bugs. But automated memory-management methods consume computing resources in deciding which portions of memory to free, resulting in slower programs, uneven performance, stalls, and other inefficiencies. For example, incrementing and decrementing reference counts every time that a reference is created or destroyed can impede a program's performance significantly.

Writing manual memory-management code is tedious and hard to do, but doing it right results in the efficient use of memory. If that's your goal, then use a lower-level language that lets you manage memory manually. On the other hand, we don't have to worry about memory as much as we did in decades past. You might opt to be more productive by writing code faster in a higher-level language that manages memory for you.

Algorithms

An algorithm is a series of steps to solve a specific problem. An algorithm sounds similar to a program, but algorithms achieve narrower goals than entire programs do. An algorithm might describe how to sort elements in a list, search for a word in a string, calculate the square root of a number, or determine whether two line segments intersect. You can find simple algorithms for calculating factorials and the Fibonacci sequence in "The while Statement" on page 46.

One of the simplest algorithms finds the largest number in a list of numbers in random order. If the list has n numbers, then finding the maximum value requires $n - 1$ comparisons: examine each number in the list in turn and keep track of the largest number seen so far. In the following pseudocode, the list resides in the array list.

```
max = list[0]
for i = 1 to list.length - 1
  if list[i] > max then
    max = list[i]
return max
```

You can implement this algorithm in any programming language. In JavaScript, the code is:

```
var list = [3, 1, 4, 5, 2];
var max = list[0];
for (var i = 1; i < list.length - 1; i++) {
  if (list[i] > max) {
    max = list[i];
  }
}
alert(max);    // 5
```

This algorithm can be easily modified to find the smallest number in a list. But there's no reason to write these functions yourself because JavaScript already provides them: Math.max() and Math.min() (page 30).

Every task can be accomplished in multiple ways. Is there another algorithm that finds the largest number in a list? Yes. Sort the list in descending (largest-to-smallest) order and then return the first item in the sorted list. But sorting is computationally more expensive than the simple method given above, so we prefer the former algorithm.

Sorting Algorithms Sampler

Bead sort
Binary tree sort
Block sort
Bubble sort
Bucket sort
Burstsort
Circle sort
Cocktail sort
Comb sort
Counting sort
Cubesort
Cycle sort
Flashsort
Gnome sort
Heapsort
Insertion sort
Introsort
Library sort
Merge sort
Odd-even sort
Pancake sort
Patience sort
Permutation sort
Pigeonhole sort
Postman sort
Quicksort
Radix sort
Selection sort
Shell sort
Sleep sort
Smoothsort
Spaghetti sort
Spreadsort
Stooge sort
Strand sort
Timsort
Tournament sort
Unshuffle sort

Sorting, in fact, is one of the most studied areas in the field of algorithms. Newcomers to programming are usually surprised at the number of ways to sort a list. Some of these algorithms are familiar. The insertion sort, for example, is used (unknowingly) by most card players to sort the cards in their hand. And some are wretched. The bubble sort, once widely taught in introductory computer science classes, is one of the worst sorts ever conceived (my initial experience as a student involved staring at the algorithm trying to figure out why it worked at all).

Sorting algorithms are classified by computational complexity (worst, average, and best behavior in terms of the size of the list), memory usage, stability, general method, and other technical criteria. Some sorts are efficient for only short lists. Some work best if the list is already nearly sorted. Some are general-purpose sorts. Search online for the name of a well-known sort to find instructional videos that demonstrate how the algorithm works step by step.

Fortunately, sorting functions are already built in to most languages. The sort() method in JavaScript, for example, sort the elements of an array. These built-in functions have been debugged, tested, and used extensively, so there's rarely a reason to write your own sorting function. If you peek behind the scenes at the source code of a built-in sorting function, then you might find that it uses, say, an insertion sort for short lists and quicksort for long lists.

In programming, there's never only one way to solve a problem. If you give ten experienced programmers the same (nontrivial) problem, then you're likely to get ten different solutions. When you're solving a problem, the first method that comes to mind might work, but don't expect it to be the best choice. Suppose that you want to calculate the nth term in the Fibonacci sequence. The code in "The while Statement" on page 46 is straightforward but hopelessly slow for large n. A simple but nonobvious algorithm involving matrix exponentiation is much faster. The simplest algorithms to conceive aren't necessarily the most efficient. Highly efficient algorithms can be quite hard to create, understand, implement, and maintain. Programming often involves tradeoffs between ease of understanding, ease of use, ease of development, speed, efficiency, and elegance.

Multithreading

You're already familiar with multitasking, the concurrent operation by one central processing unit (CPU) of multiple tasks, also called processes. An operating system that's running multiple applications and services is multitasking, for example. Multithreading extends the concept of multitasking into programs, letting you distribute separate tasks within a single program to individual threads. Each thread can run in parallel. The operating system divides processing time not only among different programs, but also among all the threads within those programs.

Multithreading is often used to maintain a program's responsiveness. You don't want your program to stall or freeze, however briefly, when a user clicks a button or prints a document. Multithreaded programs can also operate faster on systems that have multiple CPUs because independent threads naturally lend themselves to parallel execution.

A single-threaded program has only a main execution thread, like a single conveyor belt processing one instruction at a time. With multithreading, you can create additional, secondary threads that branch off the main thread and operate in parallel to it.

Threads can run independently but they can also share resources, so programmers impose restrictions that, say, prevent two different threads from saving to the same file or using the same counter variable. It's a common practice to allow only the main thread to change the user interface.

Many programming languages support multithreading in some capacity, including Java, C#, Visual Basic .NET, Python, Ruby, and many implementations of C and C++. In JavaScript, web workers provide a means for web content to run scripts in background threads without interfering with the user interface.

CHAPTER 13

Next Steps

Choosing a Language

Now that you understand the basic concepts and practices of programming, you're ready to leave the nest and explore the languages. Learning a programming language is like learning a musical instrument. You can read about it and watch tutorial videos, but there's no substitute for hands-on practice. Pick a project that interests you, and then choose a suitable language. Start small to reduce frustration. Remember that high-level languages like Python, Ruby, and JavaScript are much easier to learn than low-level languages like assembly language and C (which require intermediate to advanced programming skills and hardware knowledge to use effectively). If you want to learn object-oriented programming, start with Java or Ruby. For an overview of a language, read its Wikipedia page (*wikipedia.org*). After you install a compiler or interpreter, run the "Hello, world!" program (page 6) as a quick test. The type of project often restricts your choice of language:

- To write macOS or iOS applications, use Swift or Objective-C.

- To write Windows applications, use a .NET ("dot net") language such as C# or Visual Basic .NET.

- To write web applications, use JavaScript.

- The most popular video games are written in compiled procedural or object-oriented languages such as C or C++. Many games aren't written in a single language and include pieces written in assembly language, Java, or scripting languages.

- To write programs that you can move easily across various platforms, use a high-level scripting language like Python, Perl, or Ruby.

- To write fast, compact programs, use C or assembly language.

- To write statistical, scientific, engineering, or numerical analysis programs, use C, C++, R, Python, or Fortran.

Suggested Resources

Suggested resources for selected languages

Language	Suggested Resources
C	Compiler: GCC (*gcc.gnu.org*)
	IDEs: The GCC compiler is built into many integrated development environments
	Book: *The C Programming Language* by Brian W. Kernighan and Dennis M. Ritchie is one of the best books written about programming and is worth reading even if you don't intend to become a C programmer
C++	Compiler: GCC (*gcc.gnu.org*)
C#, VB.NET	Website: *microsoft.com/net*
	IDE: Visual Studio (*visualstudio.com*); Visual Studio Code is free
Java	Website: *java.com*
	IDEs: Eclipse (*eclipse.org*), Netbeans (*netbeans.org*)
JavaScript	Website: *developer.mozilla.org/en/docs/Web/JavaScript*
Perl	Website: *perl.org*
PHP	Website: *php.net*
Python	Website: *python.org*
R	Website: *r-project.org*
	IDE: RStudio (*rstudio.com*)
Ruby	Websites: *ruby-lang.org* and *rubyonrails.org*
Swift, Objective-C	Website: *developer.apple.com*
	IDE: Xcode (*developer.apple.com/xcode*)

Libraries and Frameworks

All mainstream languages come with vast libraries of tested, ready-to-run code that you can link to and use in your programs. In some languages these libraries are wrapped in what are called frameworks. C# and Visual Basic .NET have the .NET framework. Java has the Java Class Library. Objective-C and Swift have the Cocoa and Cocoa Touch frameworks, for Macs and iOS devices, respectively. C has the C Standard Library. Python has the Python Standard Library. And so on.

As you gain experience, you'll realize that programming is as much about libraries as it is about languages. When you're learning C#, you might wonder whether there's a class that can help you connect to a database. It exists, but it's not part of the language itself—it's in the .NET framework, courtesy of Microsoft. If you're writing an iPhone media app in Swift, you'll find built-in audio and video player classes, written by Apple, in the Cocoa Touch framework. If your Python program needs to compress a document, you'll find modules in the Python Standard Library that can zip and unzip files. As your skills advance beyond basic syntax and you become familiar with libraries, you'll learn what you must write yourself and what has already been written for you.

Libraries can have hundreds or even thousands of classes, which can intimidate beginners. But you're not meant to learn every class any more than you're expected to read every book in a real library. You need only know how to search or navigate the library to determine whether the class you're looking for exists and, if so, how to use it in your program. Online documentation for libraries typically contains class listings, class hierarchies, descriptions, syntax, sample code, version information, cross references, and miscellaneous remarks.

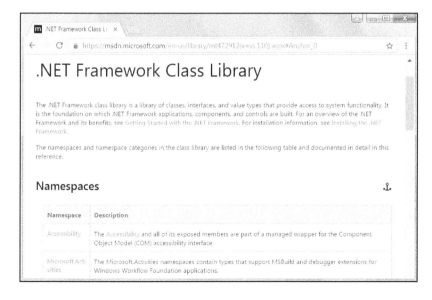

Index